JUMP Math K.1

Book K Part 1 of 2

P9-BJF-434

Contents

Put your name
or picture here!

jump math
MULTIPLYING POTENTIAL.

JUMP Math
One Yonge Street, Suite 1014
Toronto, Ontario M5E 1E5
Canada
www.jumpmath.org

Writers: Dr. Heather Betel, Julie Lorinc
Editors: Megan Burns, Liane Tsui, Julie Takasaki, Natalie Francis, Jackie Dulson, Janice Dyer, Strong Finish Editorial Design
Layout and Illustrations: Linh Lam, Fely Guinasao-Fernandes, Sawyer Paul
Cover Design: Blakeley Words+Pictures
Cover Photograph: © Photo Pegah

ISBN 978-1-928134-25-1

Second printing May 2018

Printed and bound in Canada

Welcome to JUMP Math

Entering the world of JUMP Math means believing that every child has the capacity to be fully numerate and to love math. Founder and mathematician John Mighton has used this premise to develop his innovative teaching method. The resulting resources isolate and describe concepts so clearly and incrementally that everyone can understand them.

JUMP Math is comprised of teacher's guides (which are the heart of our program), interactive whiteboard lessons, student assessment & practice books, evaluation materials, outreach programs, and teacher training. All of this is presented on the JUMP Math website: **www.jumpmath.org**.

Teacher's guides are available on the website for free use. Read the introduction to the teacher's guides before you begin using these resources. This will ensure that you understand both the philosophy and the methodology of JUMP Math. The assessment & practice books are designed for use by students, with adult guidance. Each student will have unique needs and it is important to provide the student with the appropriate support and encouragement as he or she works through the material.

Allow students to discover the concepts by themselves as much as possible. Mathematical discoveries can be made in small, incremental steps. The discovery of a new step is like untangling the parts of a puzzle. It is exciting and rewarding.

Students will need to answer the questions marked with a ▨ in a notebook. Grid paper notebooks should always be on hand for answering extra questions or when additional room for calculation is needed.

Contents

Unit 4: Patterns and Algebra: Patterns and Ordinal Numbers

Unit 5: Number Sense: Numbers 6 to 10

Unit 6: Number Sense: Comparing within 10

PART 2

Unit 7: Measurement: Comparing and Measuring

Unit 8: Number Sense: Addition within 5

Unit 9: Number Sense: Addition within 10

Unit 10: Probability and Data Management: Sorting and Graphs

Unit 11: Geometry: Solid Shapes

Unit 12: Patterns and Algebra: Patterns and Probability

Unit 13: Number Sense: Subtraction within 5

Unit 14: Number Sense: Subtraction within 10

NSK-I The I to 10 Count Sequence

☐ Colour.

I.

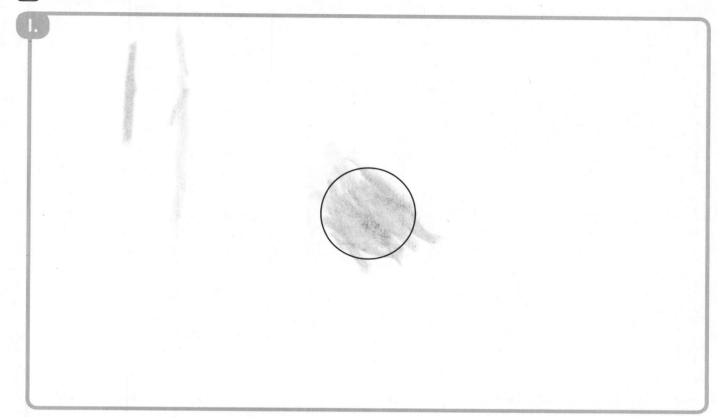

2.

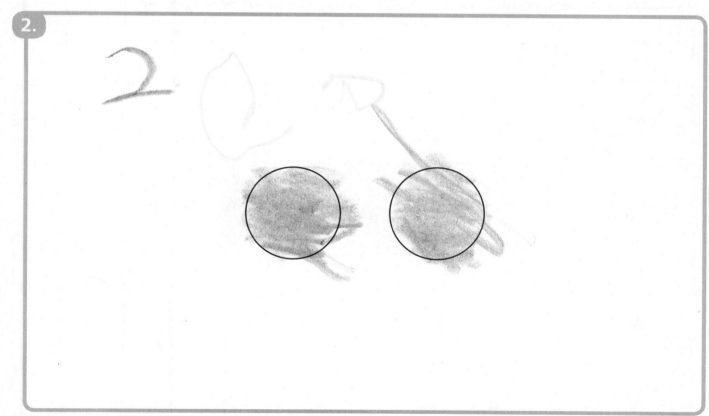

☐ Colour.

3.

4.

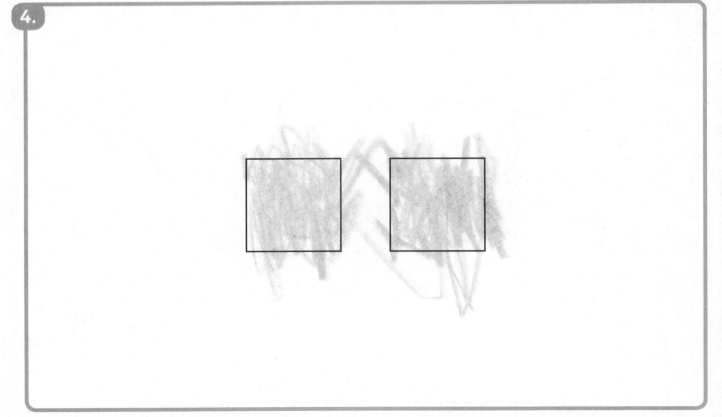

☐ Colour.

5. BONUS

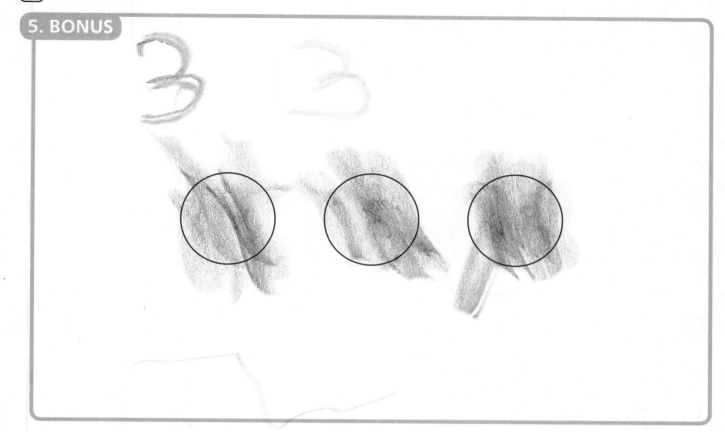

6. BONUS

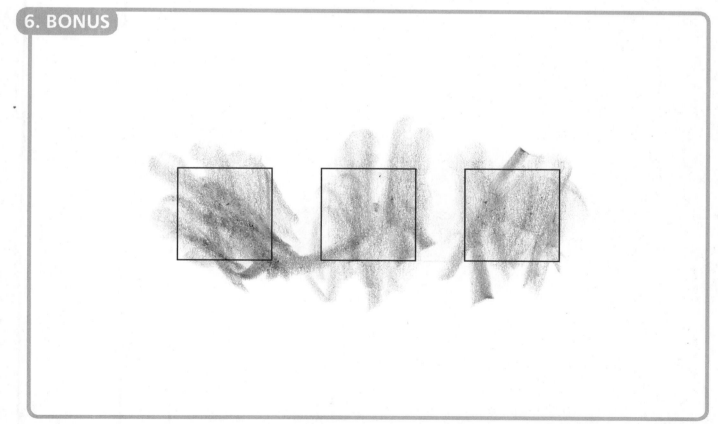

NSK-2 The Numbers 1 and 2

☐ Glue the number 1 or 2.

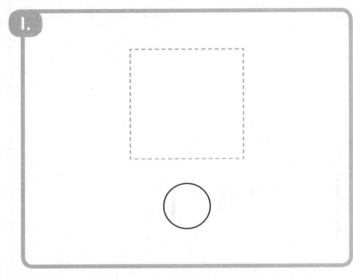

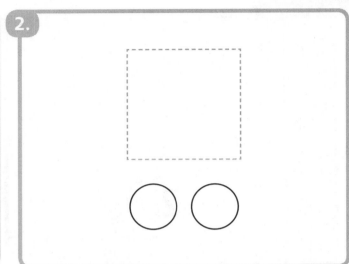

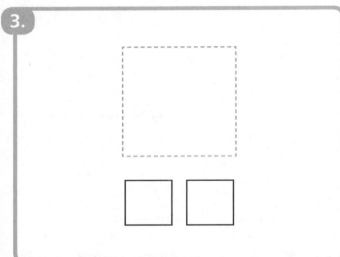

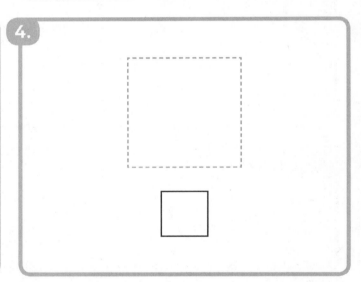

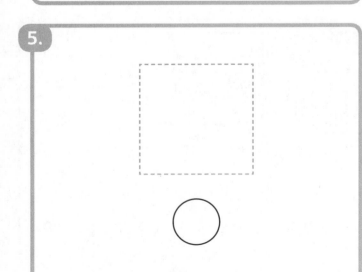

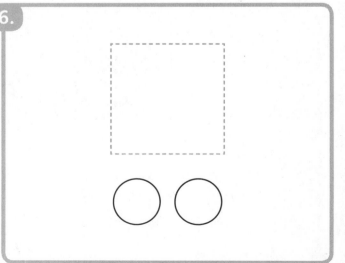

☐ Glue a picture of 1 or 2.

7.

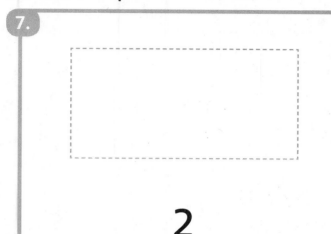

2

8.

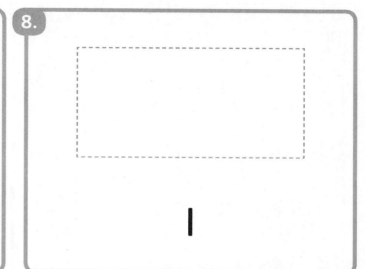

1

9.

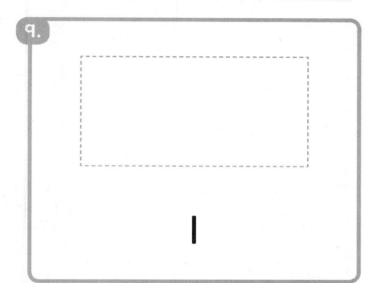

1

10.

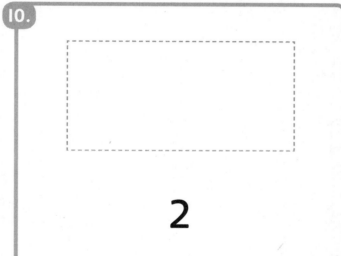

2

11.

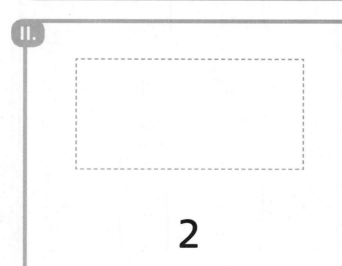

2

12.

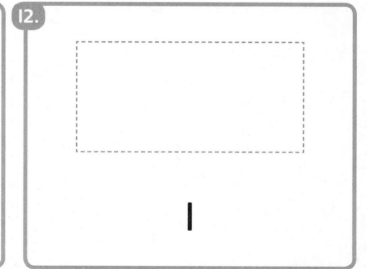

1

☐ **BONUS:** Colour 🙂 for match. Colour ☹ for no match.

13.

14.

15.

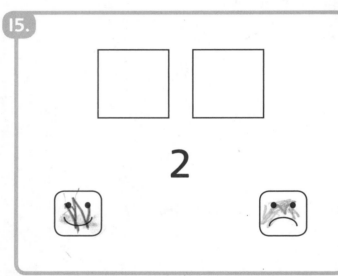

16.

17.

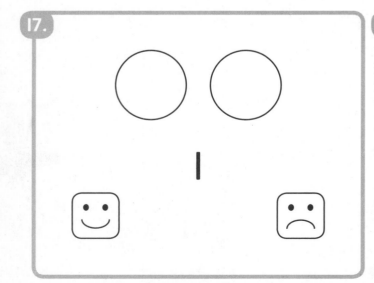

18.

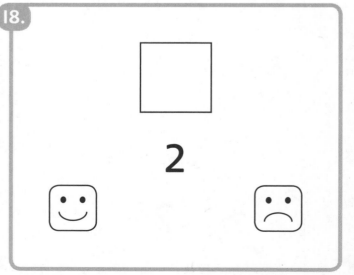

NSK-3 The Number 3

☐ Glue the number 1, 2, or 3.

1.

2.

3.

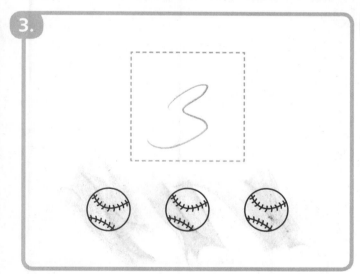

4.

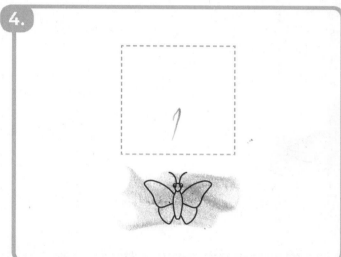

5.

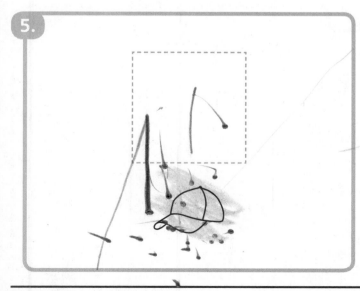

6.

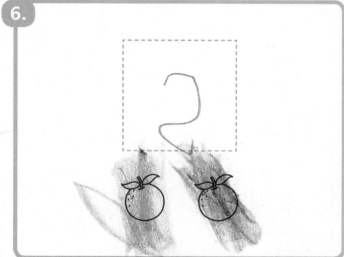

☐ Glue a picture of 1, 2, or 3.

7.

2

8.

1

9.

3

10.

2

11.

1

12.

3

☐ BONUS: Colour 🙂 for correct. Colour 🙁 for not correct.

13.

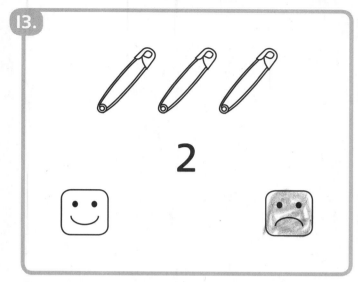

2

🙂   🙁

14.

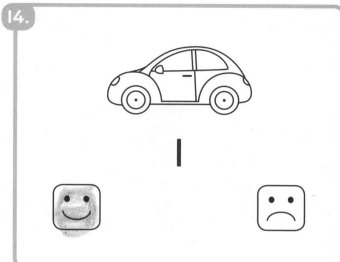

1

🙂   🙁

15.

1

🙂   🙁

16.

3

🙂   🙁

17.

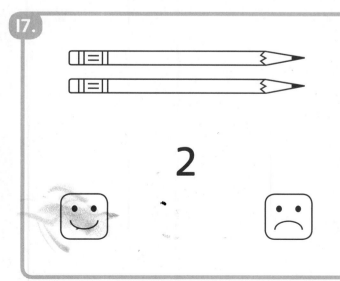

2

🙂   🙁

18.

3

🙂   🙁

NSK-4 Counting

☐ Count.

1.

2.

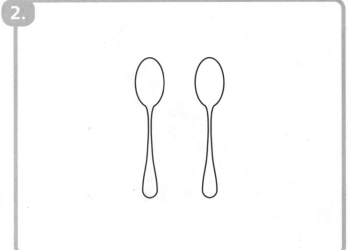

3.

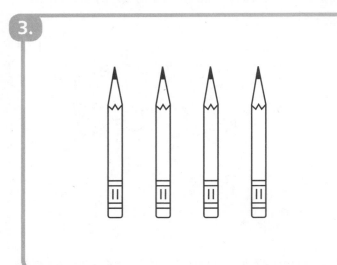

4.

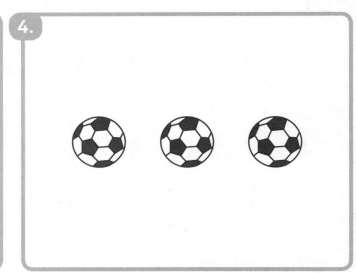

5.

6.

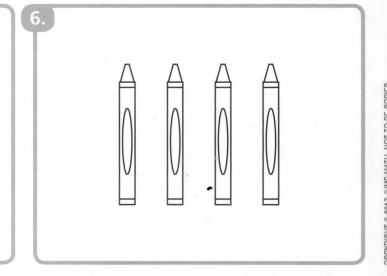

☐ Count.

7.

8.

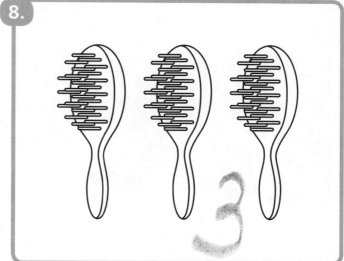

3

9.

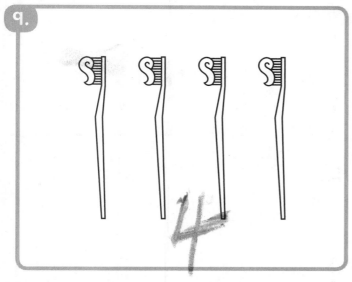

4

10.

11.

12.

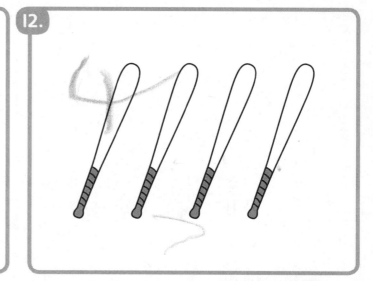

4

NSK-5 Counting 1, 2, and 3

☐ Use ⬤. Count.

1.

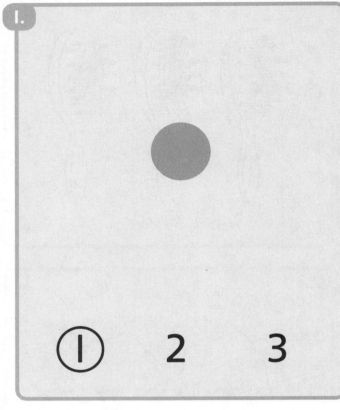

①   2   3

2.

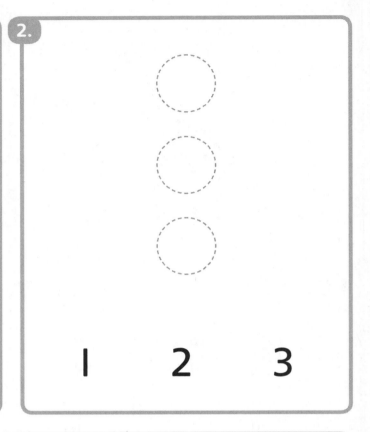

1   2   3

3.

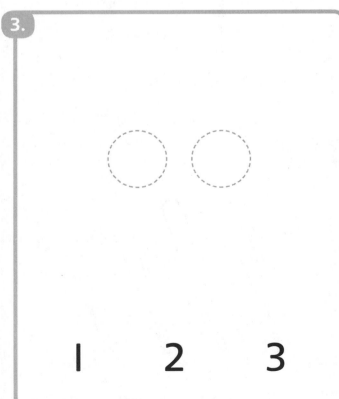

1   2   3

4.

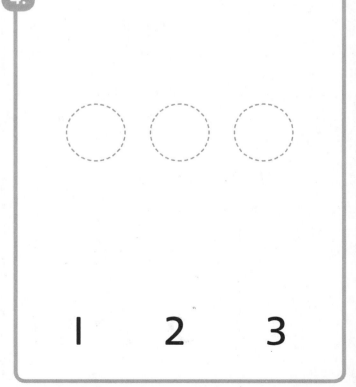

1   2   3

☐ Use ●. Count.

5.

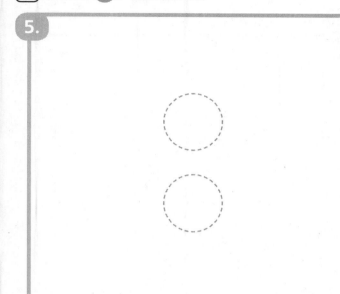

1   2   3

6.

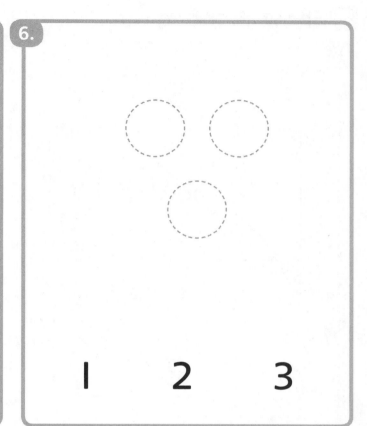

1   2   3

7.

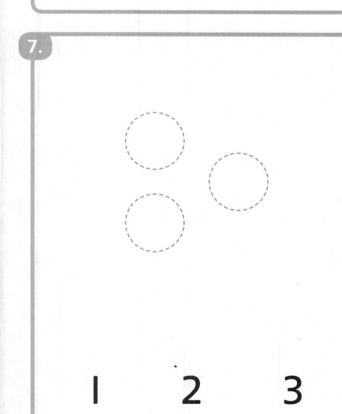

1   2   3

8.

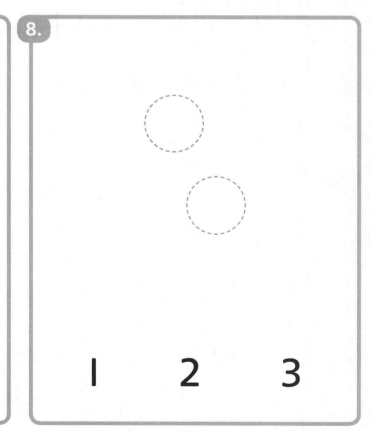

1   2   3

☐ Show counting out.

1.
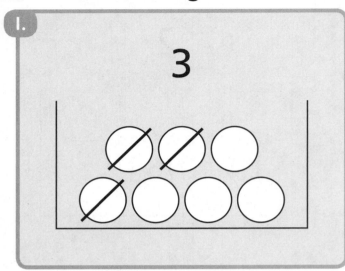

2.
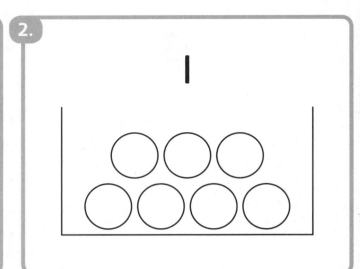

3.
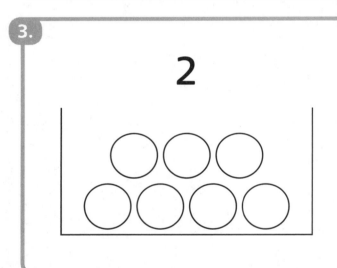

4.
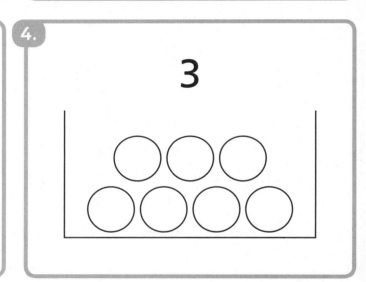

5.
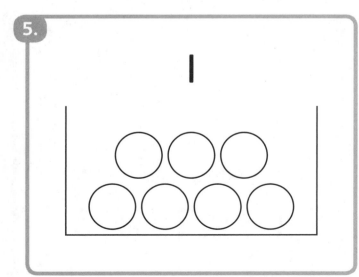

6.
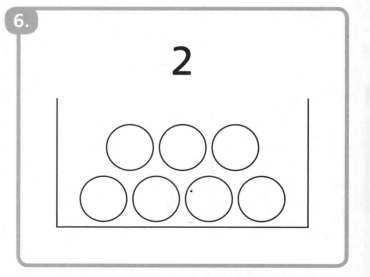

☐ **BONUS:** Show counting out.

7.

3

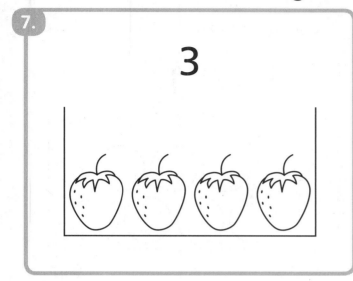

8.

2

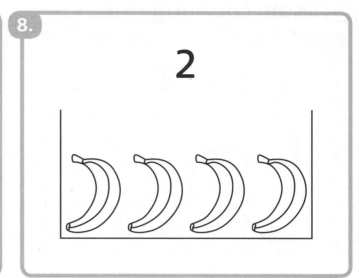

9.

1

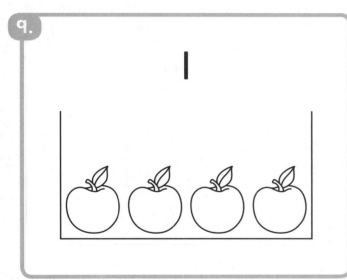

10.

3

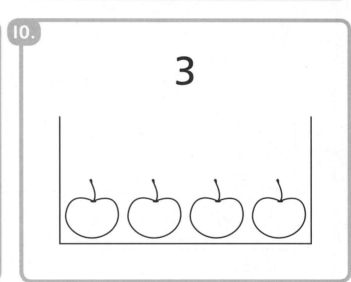

11.

2

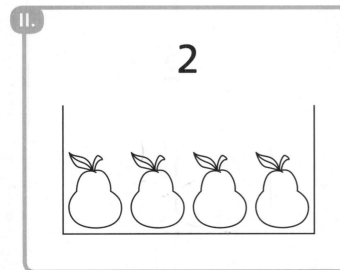

12.

1

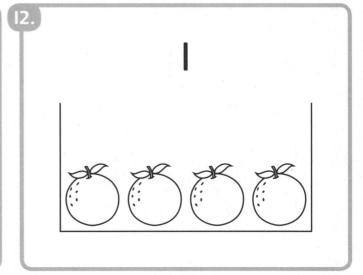

NSK-7 Writing 1, 2, and 3

☐ Trace.

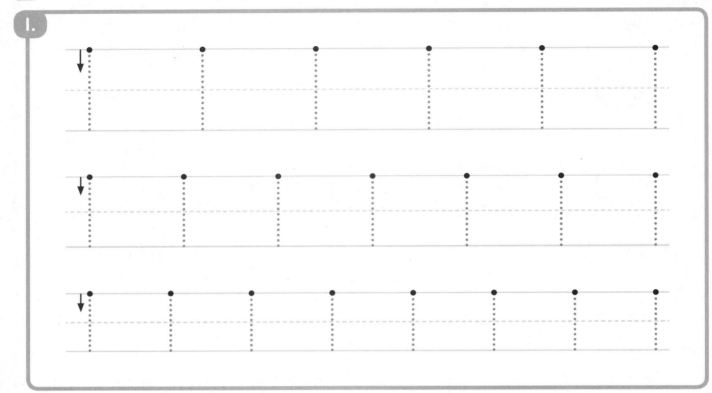

☐ Trace.

3.

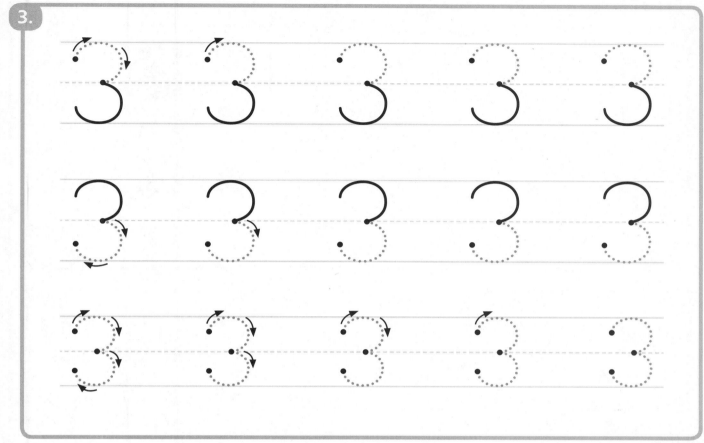

4.

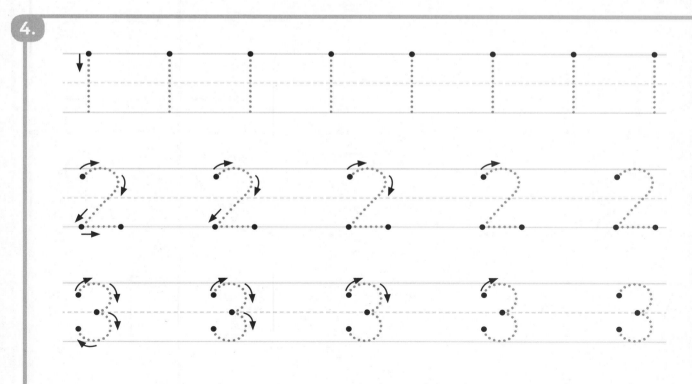

☐ Trace and colour.

5.

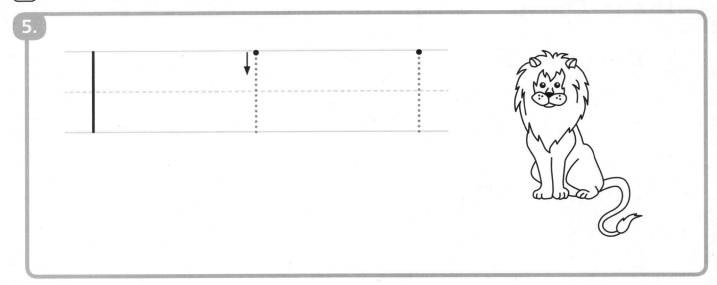

6.

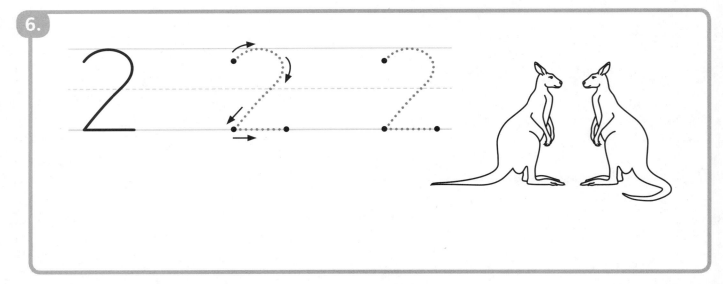

7.

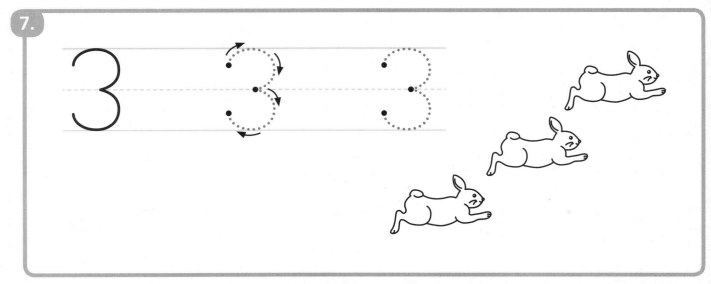

NSK-8 Counting 4

☐ Use ●. Count.

1.

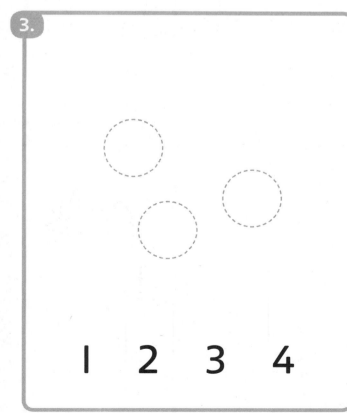

1 ② 3 4

2.

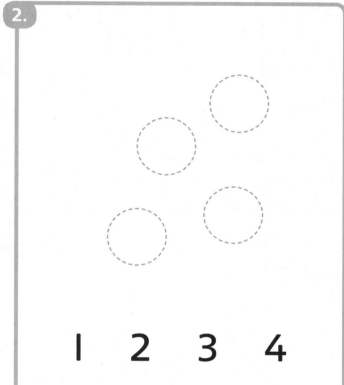

1 2 3 4

3.

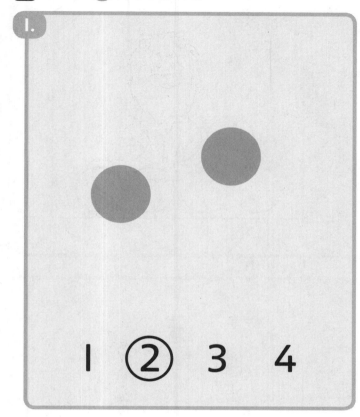

1 2 3 4

4.

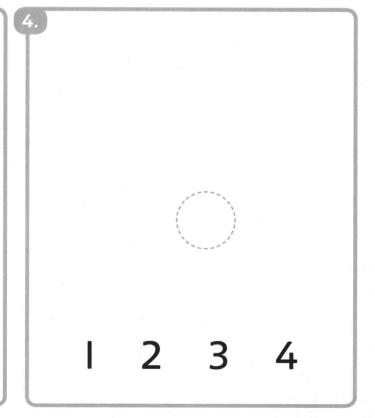

1 2 3 4

☐ Show counting out.

5.

4

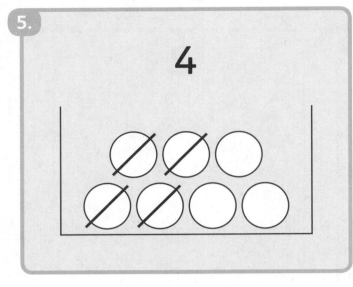

6.

2

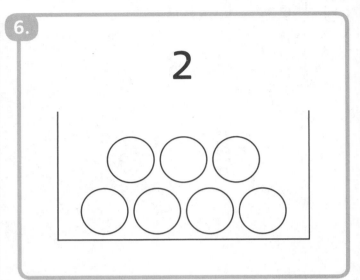

7.

1

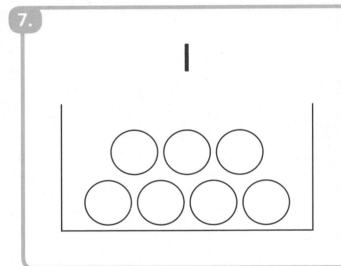

8.

3

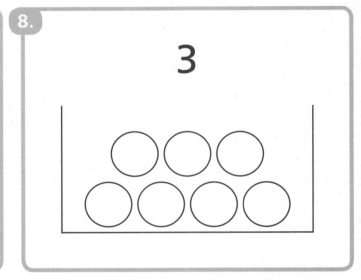

9.

3

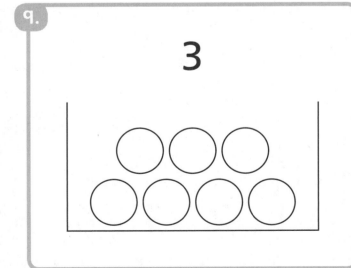

10.

4

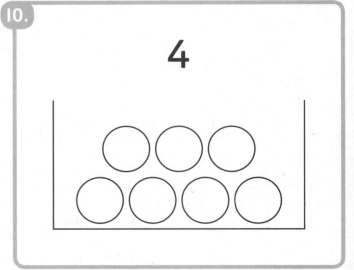

☐ **BONUS:** Show counting out.

11.

3

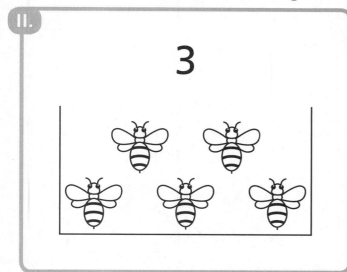

12.

2

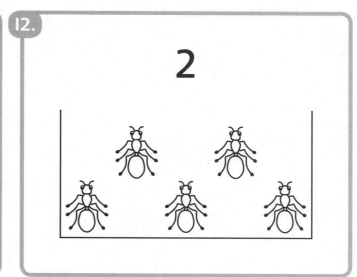

13.

4

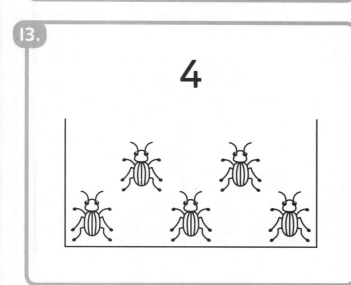

14.

1

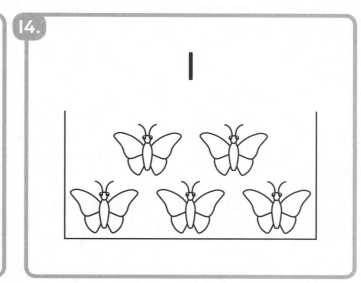

15.

3

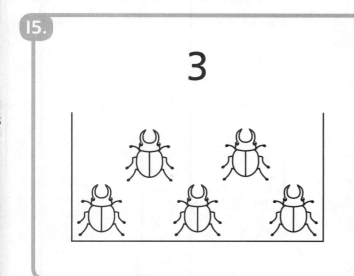

16.

4

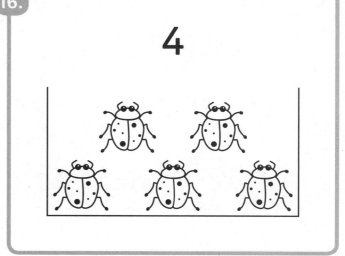

☐ Glue the number 3 or 4.

☐ Glue the number 1, 2, 3, or 4.

7.

8.
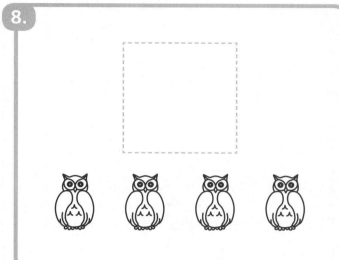

9.
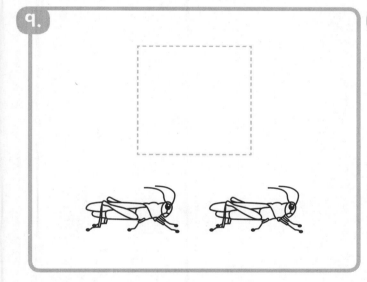

10.
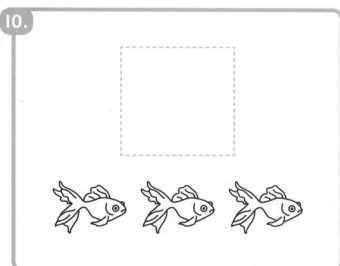

11.
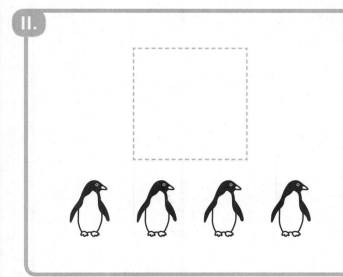

12.
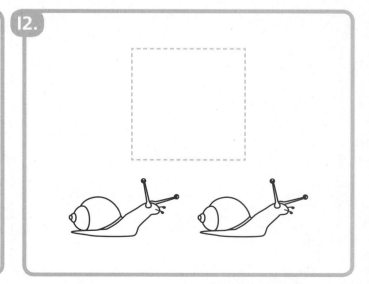

Glue a picture of 1, 2, 3, or 4.

13.

3

14.

1

15.

2

16.

4

17.

4

18.

3

NAME _____

☐ **BONUS:** Colour 🙂 for correct. Colour 🙁 for not correct.

19.

4

20.

2

21.

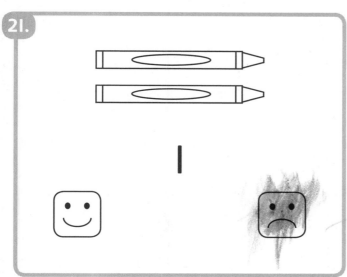

1

22.

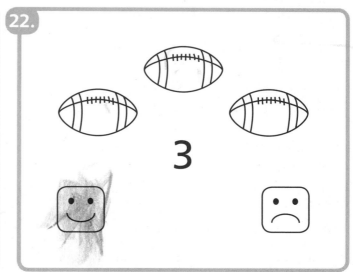

3

23.

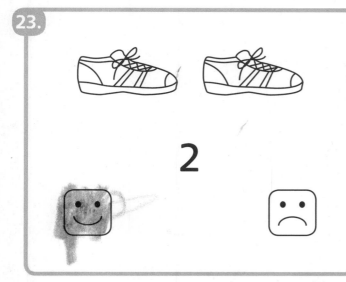

2

24.

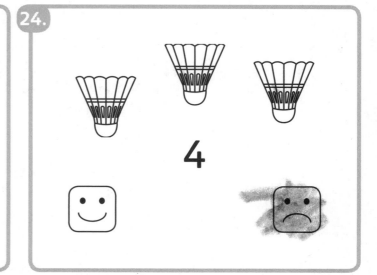

4

☐ Trace.

1.

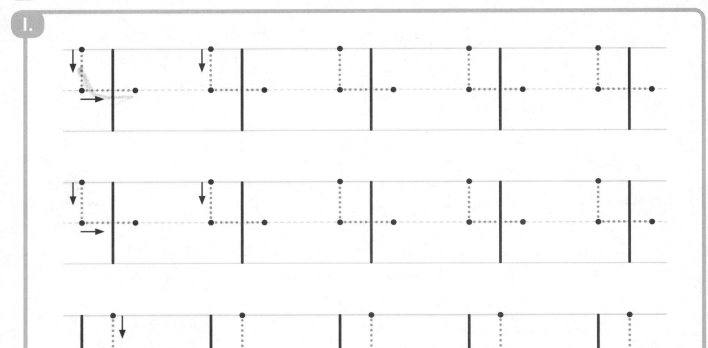

2.

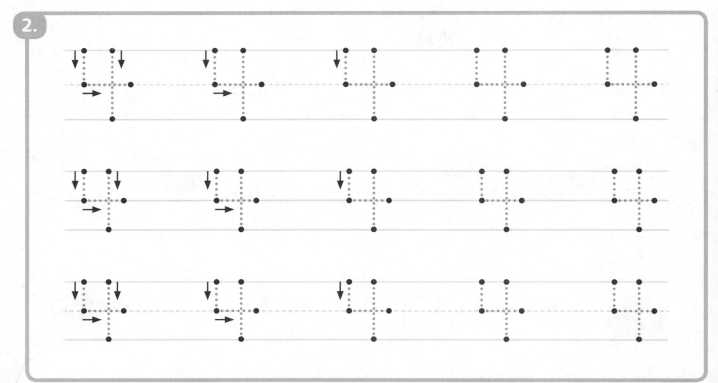

☐ Trace and colour.

3.

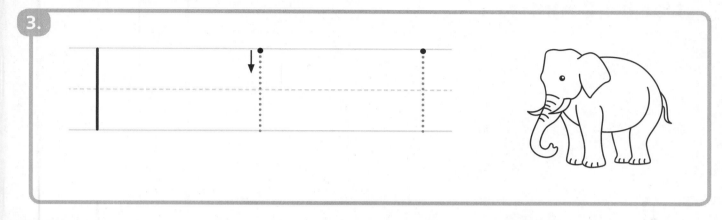

4.

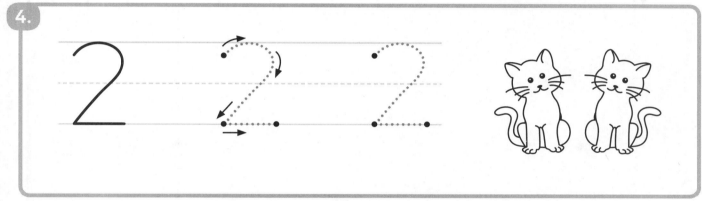

5.

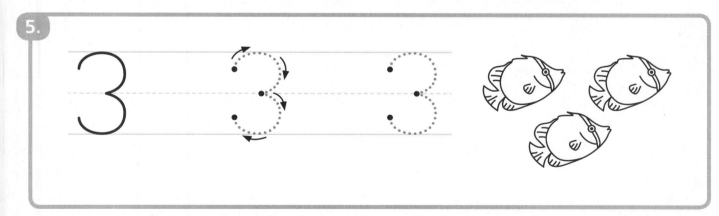

6.

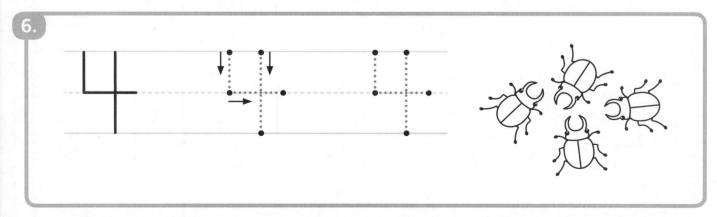

☐ Use ●. Count.

1.

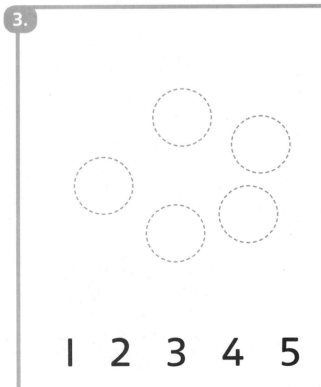

1 ② 3 4 5

2.

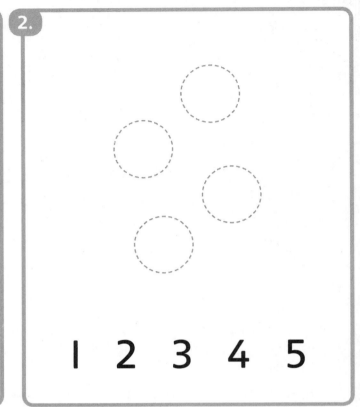

1 2 3 4 5

3.

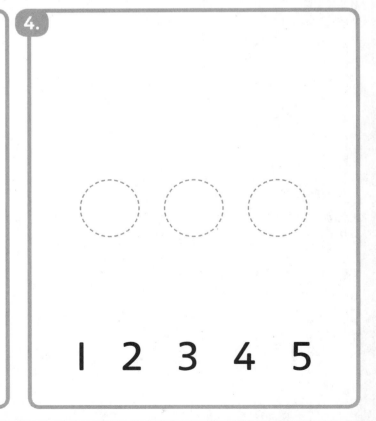

1 2 3 4 5

4.

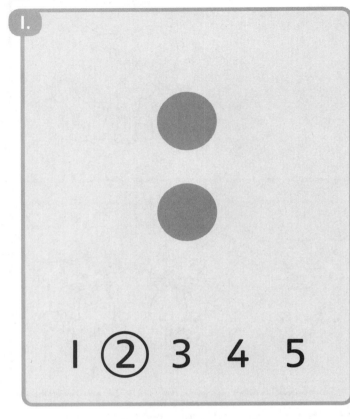

1 2 3 4 5

☐ Use ⚫. Count.

5.

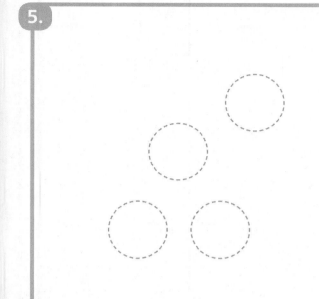

1 2 3 4 5

6.

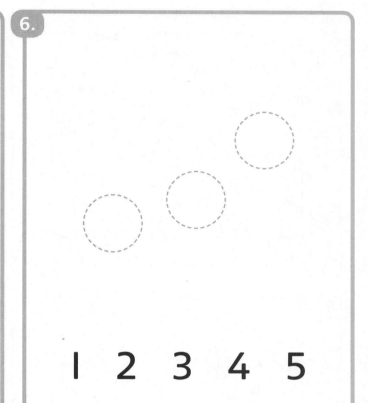

1 2 3 4 5

7.

1 2 3 4 5

8.

1 2 3 4 5

Show counting out.

9.

3

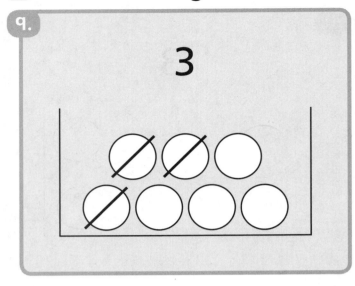

10.

5

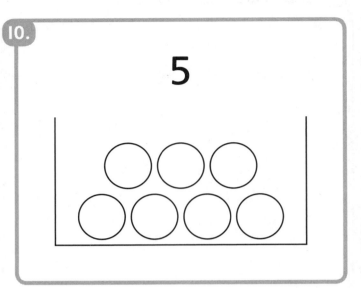

11.

2

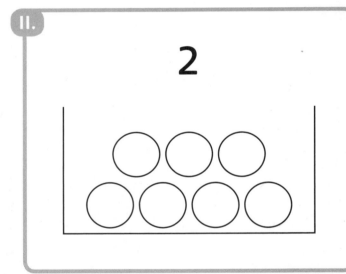

12.

4

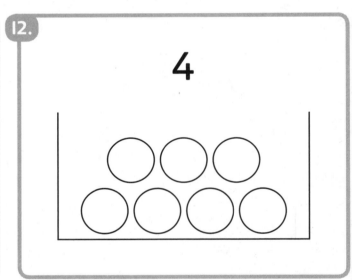

13.

5

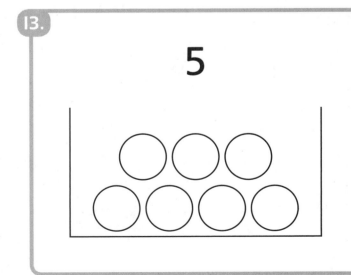

14.

1

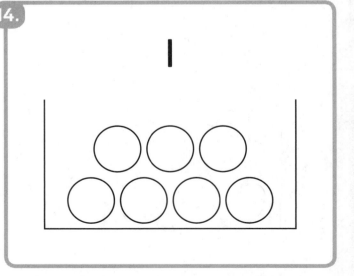

☐ **BONUS:** Show counting out.

15.

4

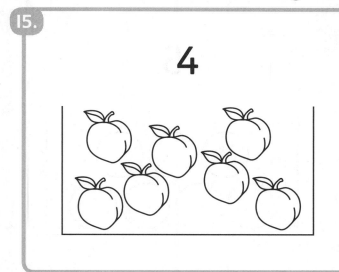

16.

3

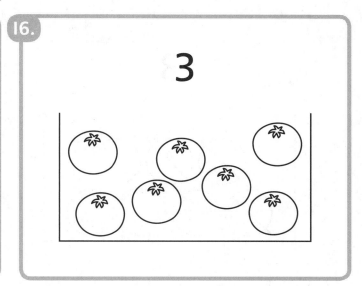

17.

5

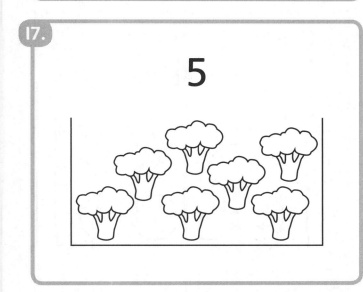

18.

2

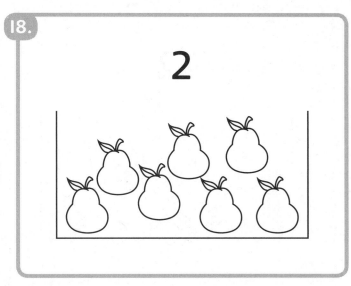

19.

3

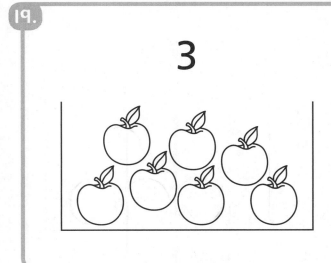

20.

5

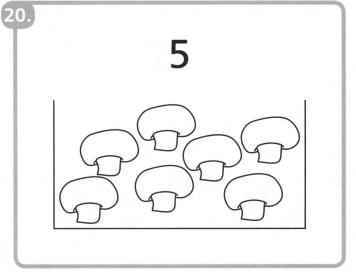

☐ Glue the number I, 2, 3, 4, or 5.

I.

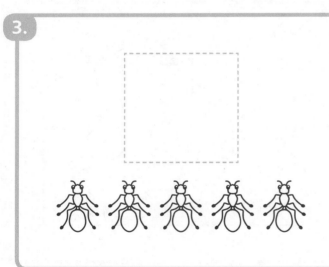

2.

3.

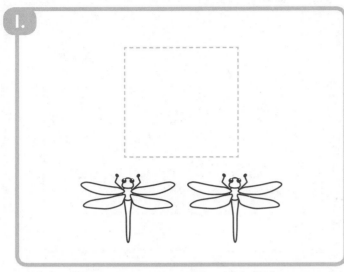

4.

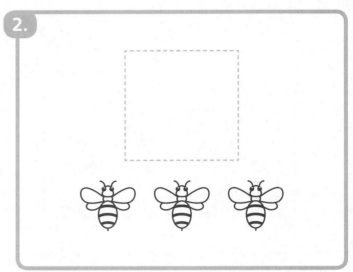

5.

6.

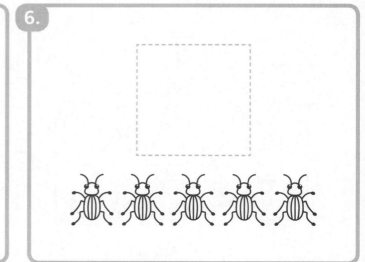

NAME _____

☐ Glue a picture of 1, 2, 3, 4, or 5.

7.
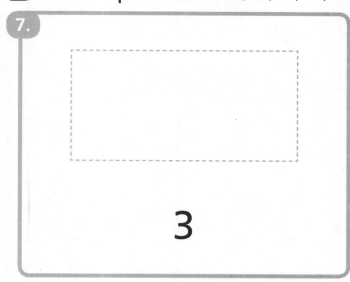

3

8.
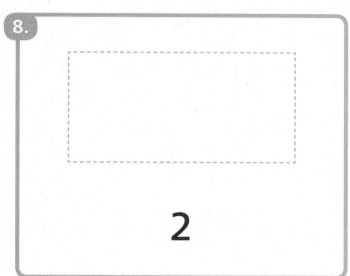

2

9.
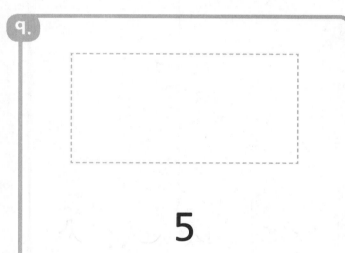

5

10.
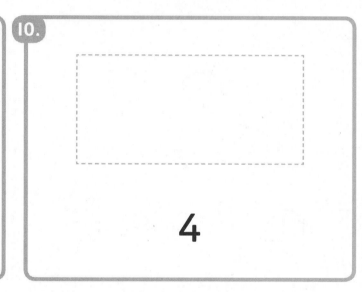

4

11.
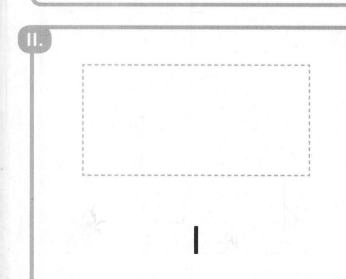

1

12.

5

13.

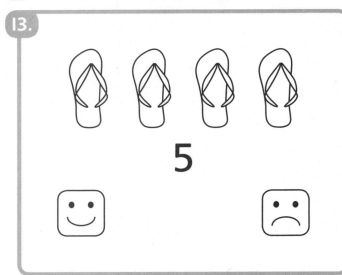

5

🙂   🙁

14.

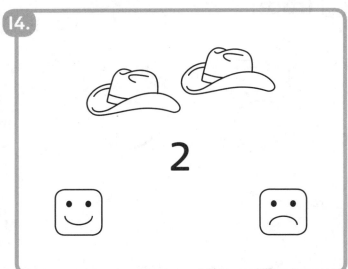

2

🙂   🙁

15.

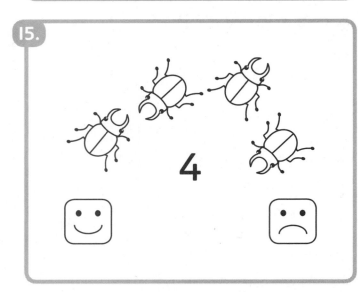

4

🙂   🙁

16.

3

🙂   🙁

17.

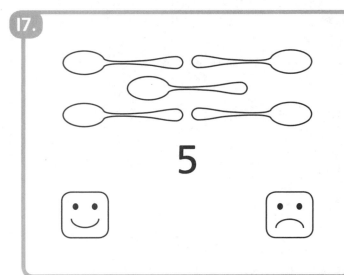

5

🙂   🙁

18.

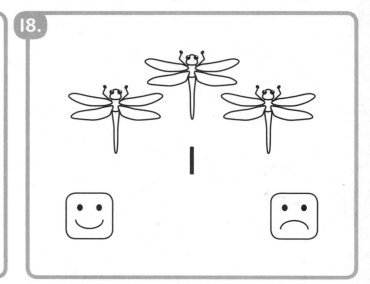

1

🙂   🙁

NSK-13 Writing 5

☐ Trace.

1.

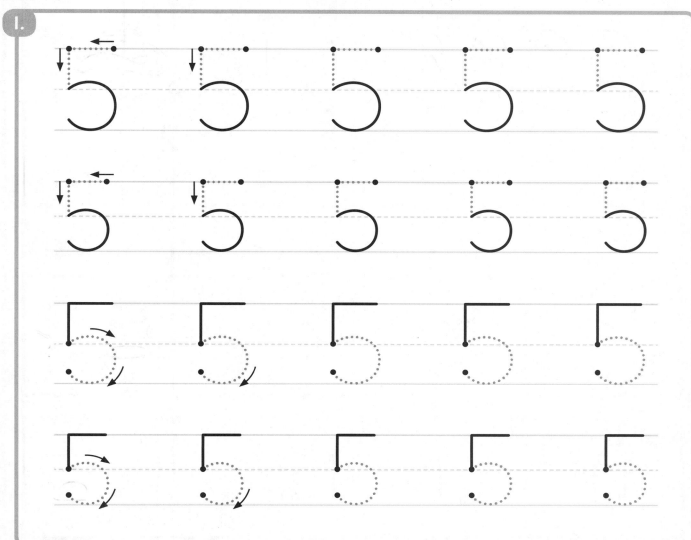

2.

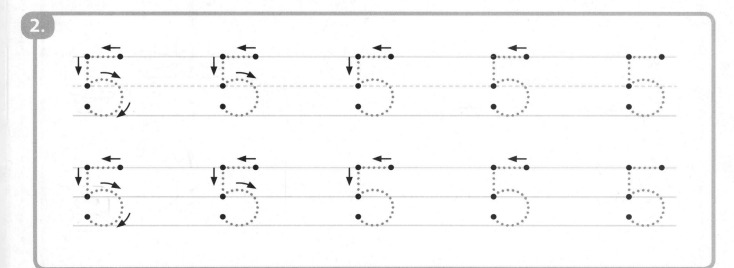

☐ Trace and colour.

3.

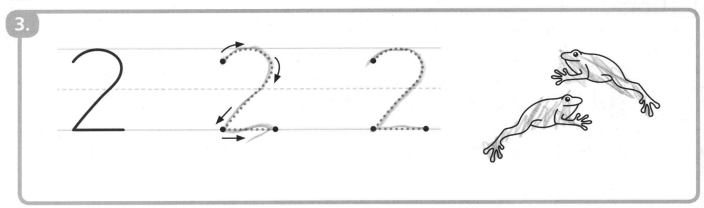

4.

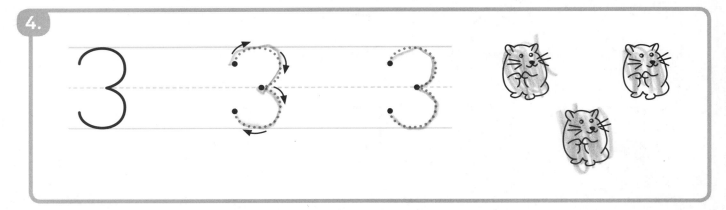

5.

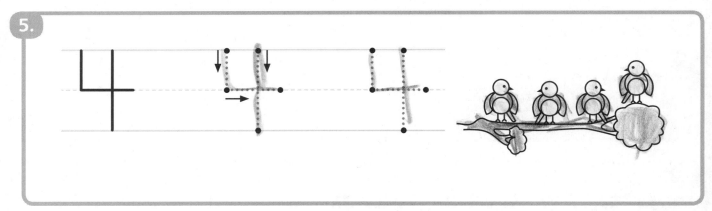

6.

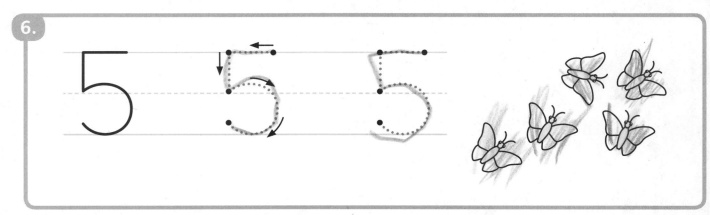

NSK-14 Review of 1, 2, 3, 4, and 5

☐ Colour.

1.

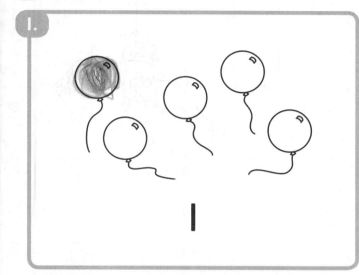

1

2.

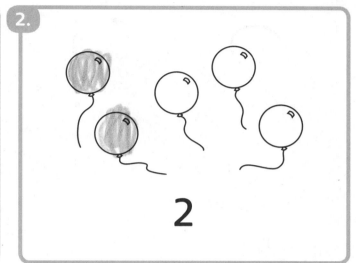

2

3.

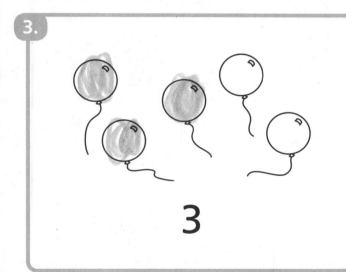

3

4.

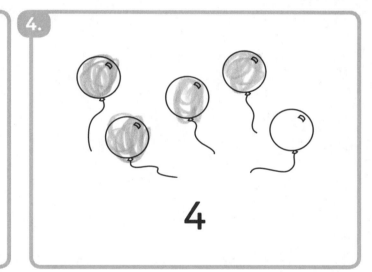

4

5.

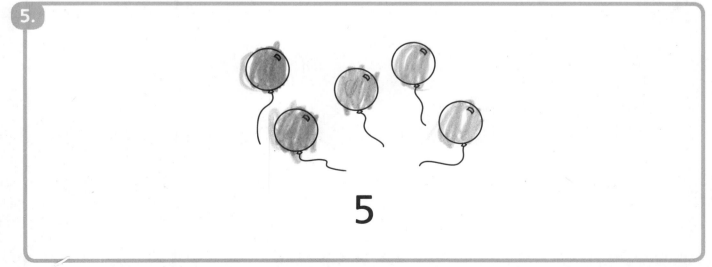

5

☐ Colour.

6.

1

7.

2

8.

3

9.

4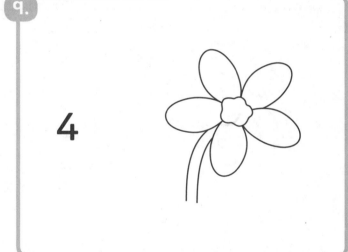

10.

5

NSK-I5 Counting to 20

☐ Trace.

1.

 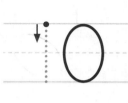 0 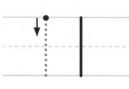 1  2

 3  4  5

 6 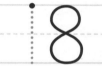 7 5 8

 9  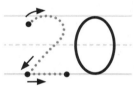 20

2.

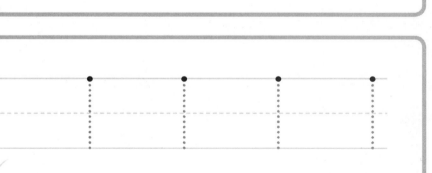

3.

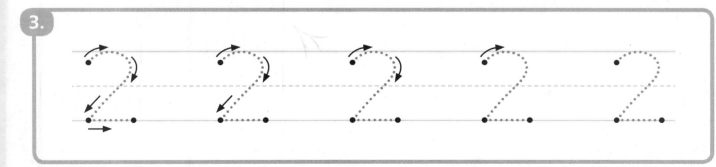

NSK-16 **More**

☐ Colour the ☼ for the group that has **more**.

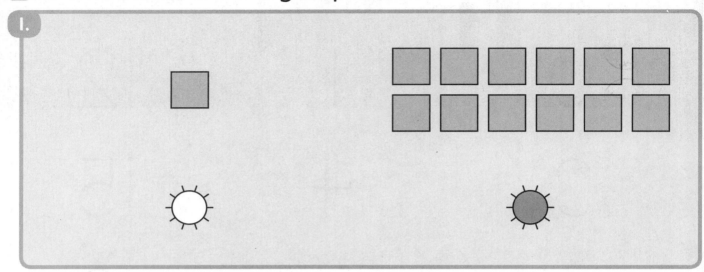

1.

2.

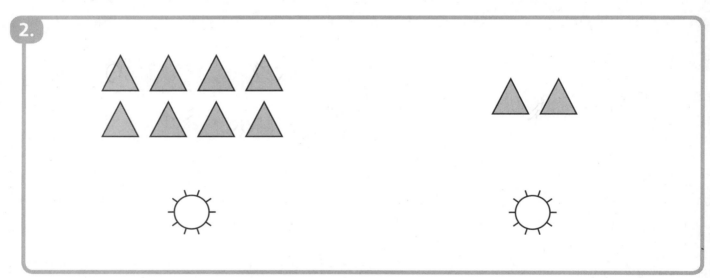

3.

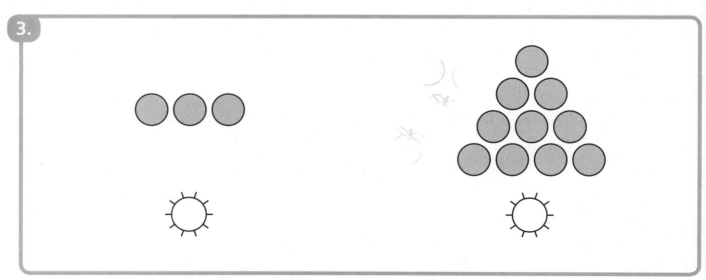

Colour the for the group that has more.

4.

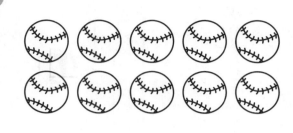

5.

6.

☐ Join the dots.

7.

8.

9.

10.

11.

12.

13.

14.

15.

16.

17.

18.

⬜ Join the dots.

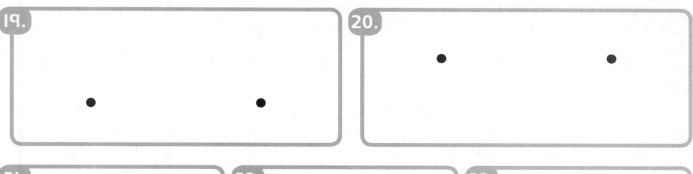

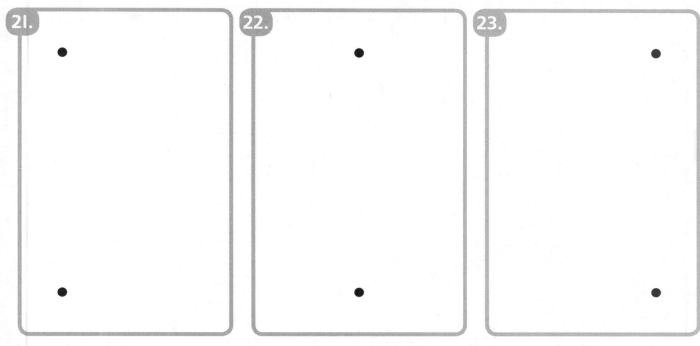

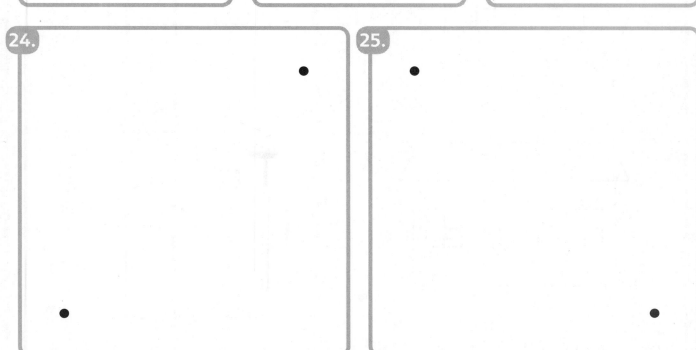

NSK-I7 The Same Number (Matching)

☐ Glue a ▯ on each ⌂.

I.

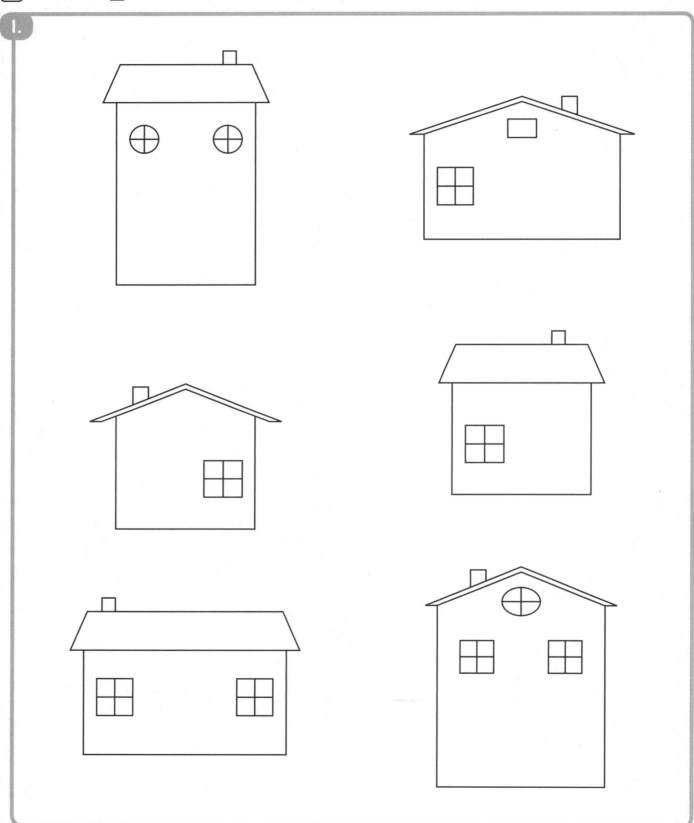

☐ Draw a line to match each  with a .

2.

 •   •

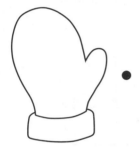 •   •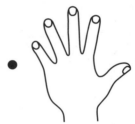

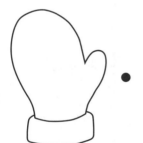 •   •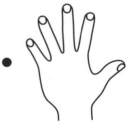

 •————————————————————•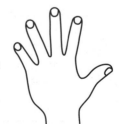

☐ Draw a line to match each 👣 with a 👟.

3.

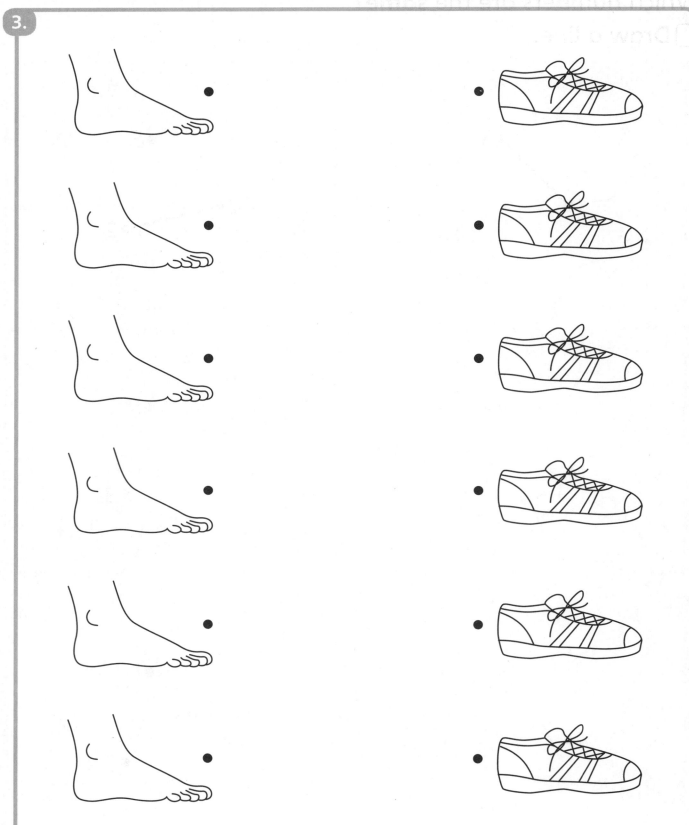

NSK-18 The Same Number (Counting)

Which numbers are the **same**?

☐ Draw a line.

1.
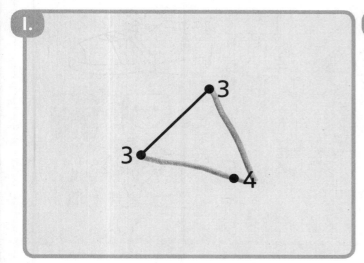

2.
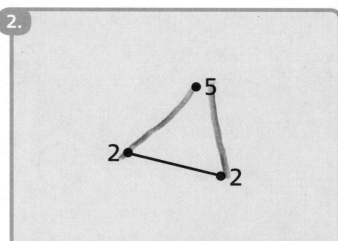

3.
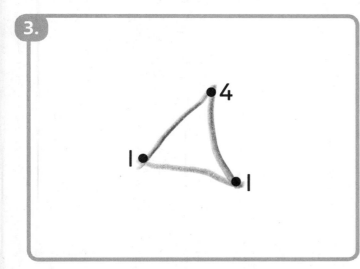

4.
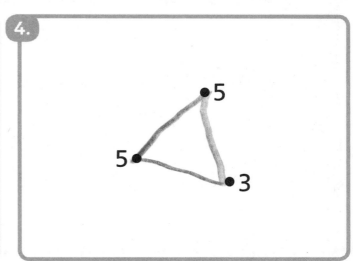

5.
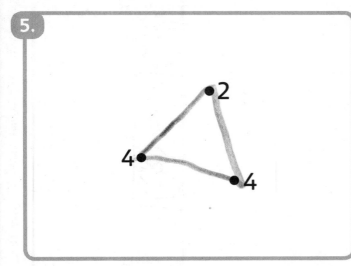

6.
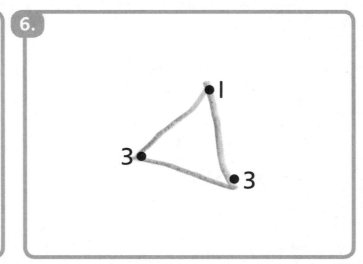

Count. Circle the number.
Colour 🙂 for the same. Colour 🙁 for not the same.

7.

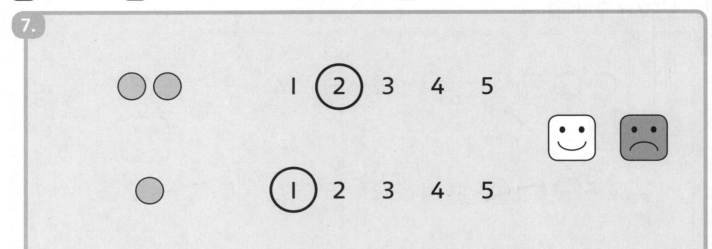

1　(2)　3　4　5

1　(1)　2　3　4　5

8.

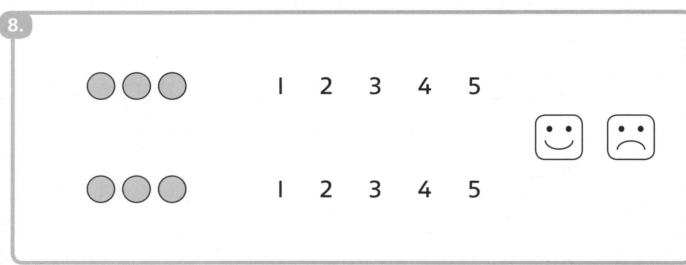

1　2　3　4　5

1　2　3　4　5

9.

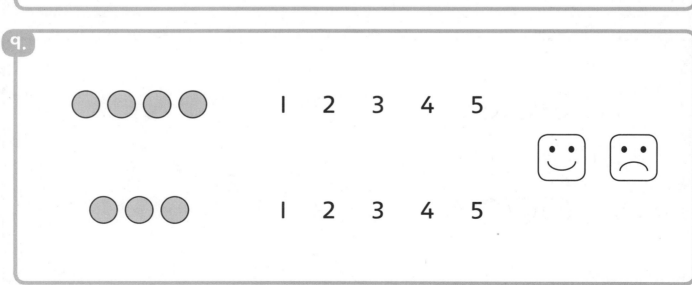

1　2　3　4　5

1　2　3　4　5

Count. Circle the number.
Colour  for the same. Colour  for not the same.

10.

◯ ◯ ◯   1   2   3   4   5

◯ ◯ ◯ ◯ ◯   1   2   3   4   5

11.

◯ ◯ ◯ ◯   1   2   3   4   5

◯ ◯   1   2   3   4   5

12.

◯ ◯ ◯ ◯ ◯   1   2   3   4   5

◯ ◯ ◯ ◯ ◯   1   2   3   4   5

☐ Match by drawing a line.
☐ Colour the ☼ on the side that has **more**.

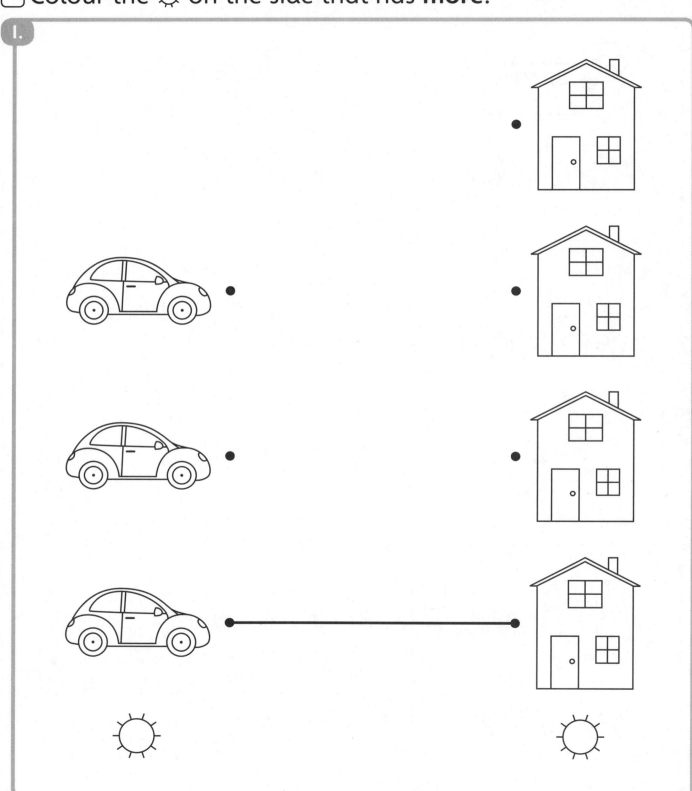

Match by drawing a line.
Colour the ☼ on the side that has more.

2.

3.

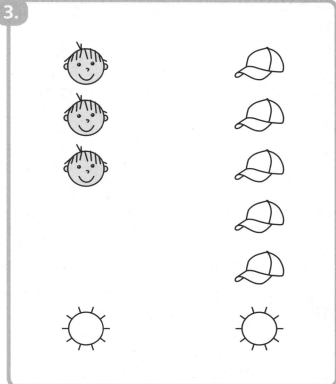

4.

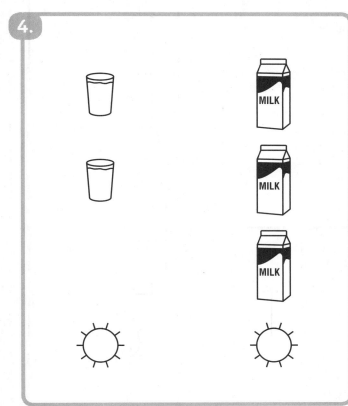

5.

1 2 3 4 5

☐ Circle the **greater** number.

1.

2   (4)

2.

(3)   1

3.

4   5

4.

2   5

5.

3   2

6.

4   3

7.

5   1

8.

1   4

☐ Count. Circle the number.
☐ Colour the for the greater number.

9.

   1   2   3   4   5

   1   2   3   4   5

10.

   1   2   3   4   5

   1   2   3   4   5

11.

   1   2   3   4   5

Count. Circle the number.
Colour the  for the greater number.

12.

● ● ● ●　　　1　2　3　4　5　　　

●　　　　　1　2　3　4　5　　　

13.

● ● ● ●　　　1　2　3　4　5　　　

● ● ● ● ●　　　1　2　3　4　5　　　

14.

● ●　　　1　2　3　4　5　　　

● ● ● ●　　　1　2　3　4　5

NSK-2I **Less Than (Matching)**

☐ Colour the ☼ for the group that has **fewer**.

I.

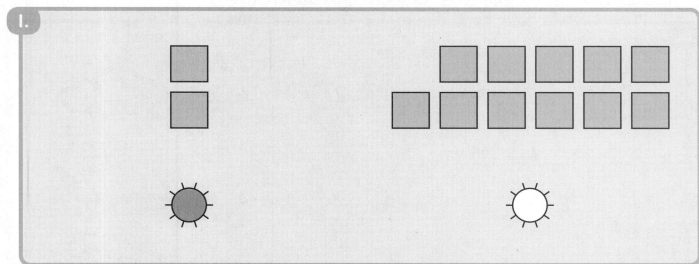

2.

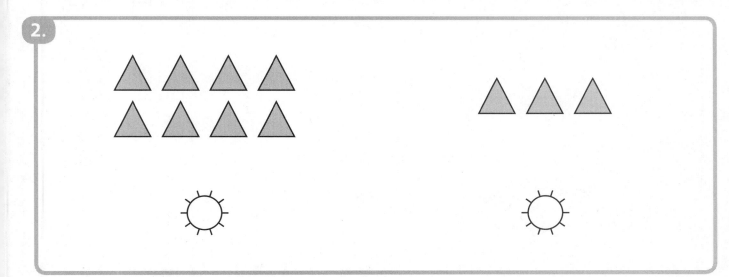

3.

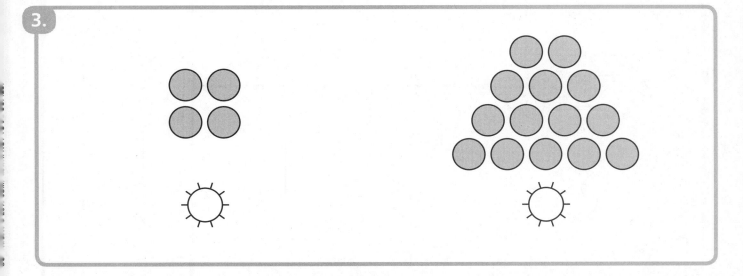

☐Match by drawing a line.
☐Colour the ☼ on the side that has fewer.

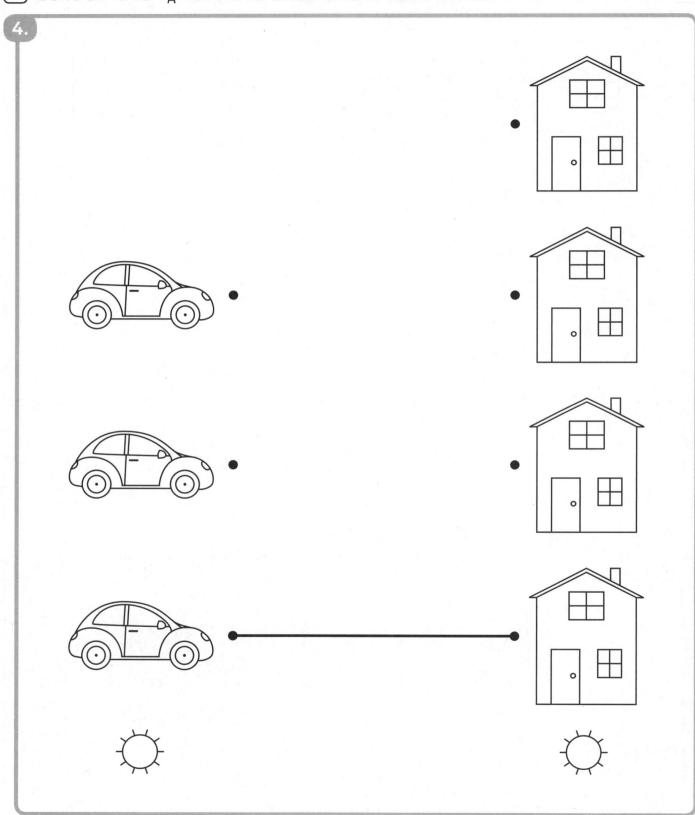

☐ Match by drawing a line.
☐ Colour the ☼ on the side that has fewer.

5.

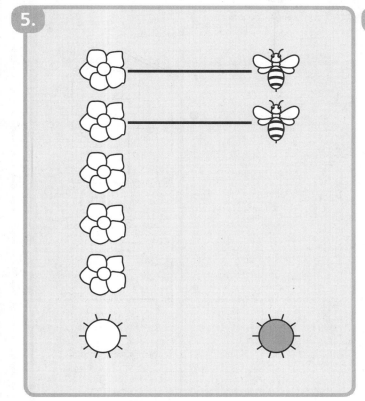

6.

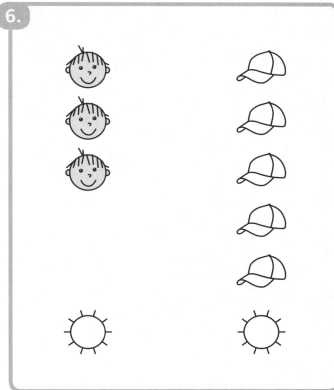

7.

8.

☐ Circle the number that is **less**.

1.
（2）   4

2.
3   （1）

3.
4   5

4.
2   5

5.
3   2

6.
4   3

7.
5   1

8.
1   4

☐ Count. Circle the number.
☐ Colour the ☼ for the number that is less.

9.

   1   2   3   4   5   ☼

   1   2   3   4   5   ☼

10.

   1   2   3   4   5   ☼

   1   2   3   4   5   ☼

11.

   1   2   3   4   5

   1   2   3   4   5   ☼

Count. Circle the number.

Colour the  for the number that is less.

12.

⬤⬤⬤⬤   1   2   3   4   5

⬤   1   2   3   4   5

13.

⬤⬤⬤⬤   1   2   3   4   5

⬤⬤⬤⬤⬤   1   2   3   4   5

14.

⬤⬤   1   2   3   4   5

⬤⬤⬤⬤   1   2   3   4   5

NSK-23 **Zero**

☐ Colour the ☼ to show which is 0.

1.

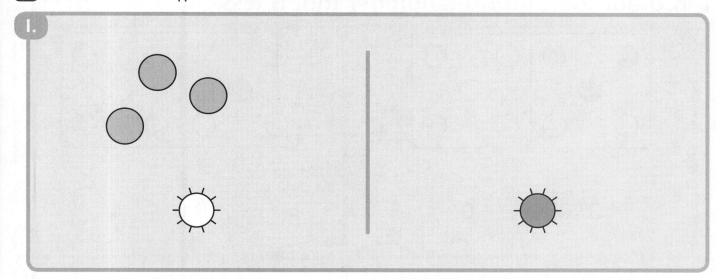

2.

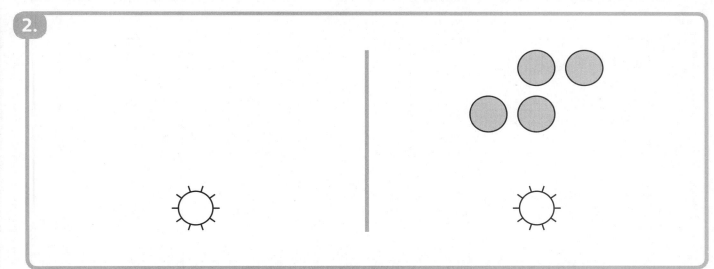

3.

Colour dots to show the numbers.

4.

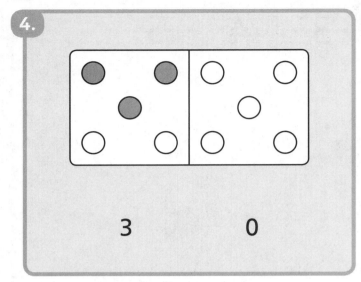

3   0

5.

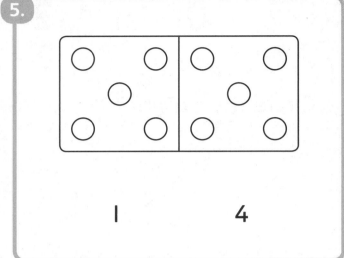

1   4

6.

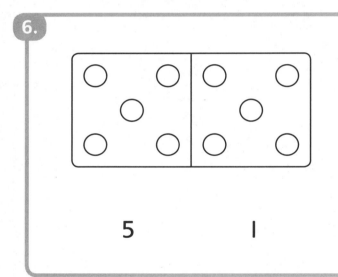

5   1

7.

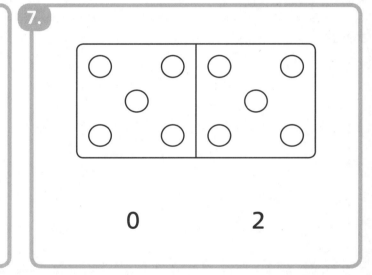

0   2

8.

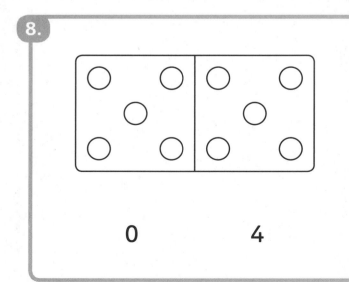

0   4

9.

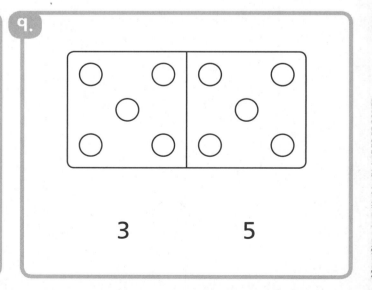

3   5

0   1   2   3   4   5

☐ Circle the number that is **less**.

10.

2   ⓪

11.

0   4

12.

0   1

13.

3   1

14.

4   0

15.

2   5

16.

4   5

17.

3   0

☐ Trace.

18.

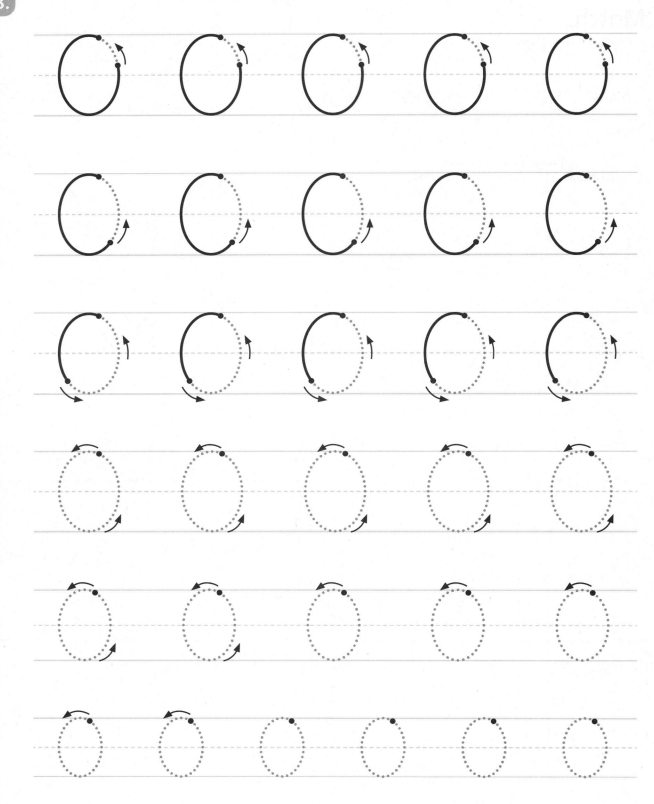

NSK-24 Comparing Numbers 1 to 5

☐ Colour to show the numbers.
☐ Match.

1.

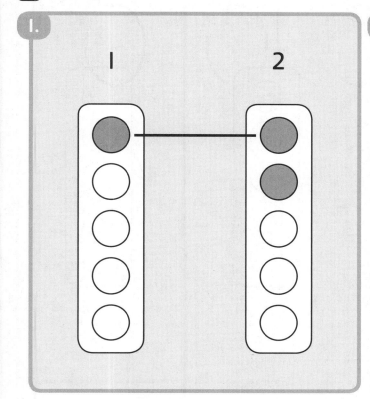

2.

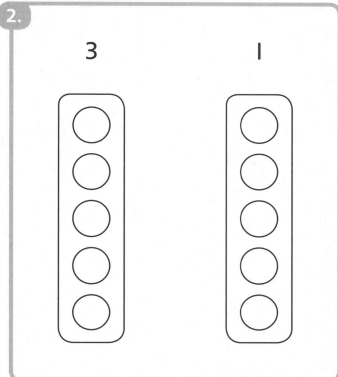

3.

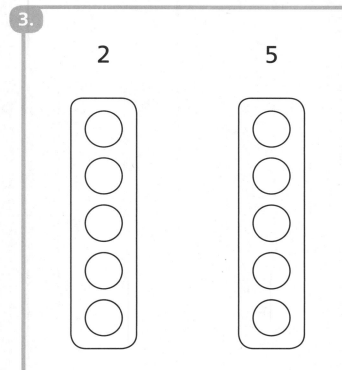

4.

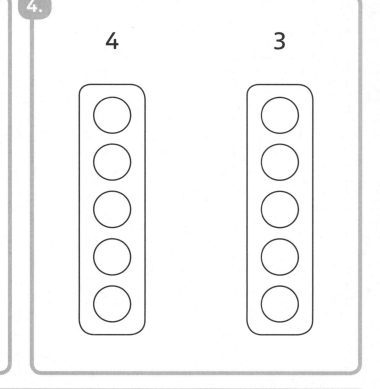

Colour to show the numbers. Match.
Colour the 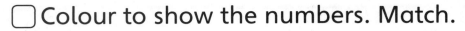 for the greater number.

5.

3   2

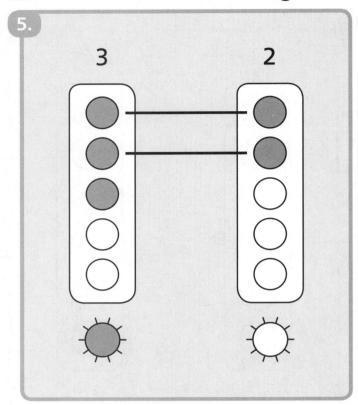

6.

1   4

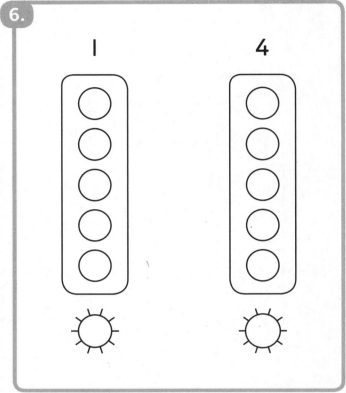

7.

5   2

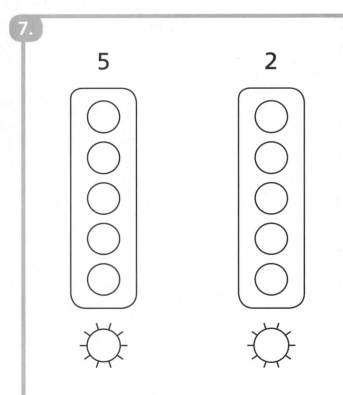

8.

3   5

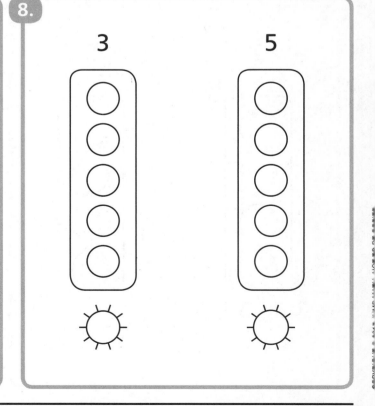

☐ Colour to show the numbers. Match.
☐ Colour the ☼ for the number that is less.

9.

3   1

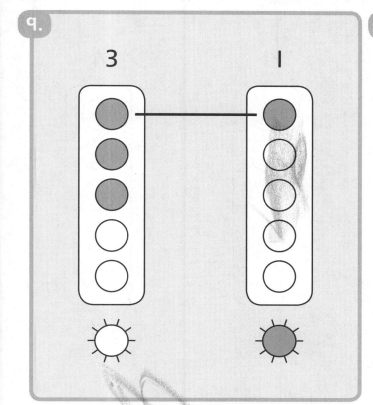

10.

2   4

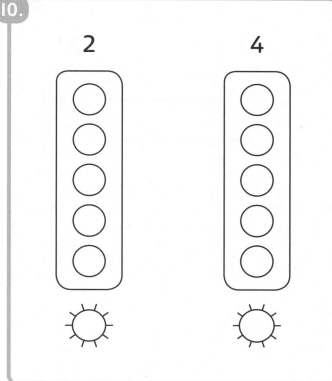

11.

5   4

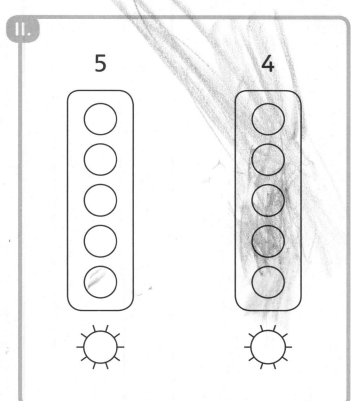

12.

2   3

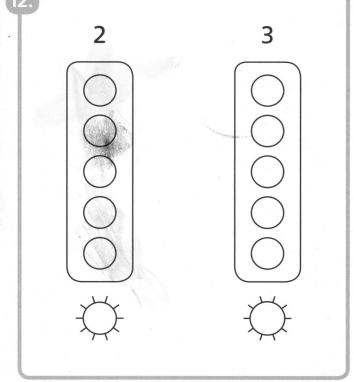

GK-I Counting to 30

☐ Trace.

1.

 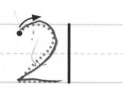 22

 24 25

26 27 8

9 30

2.

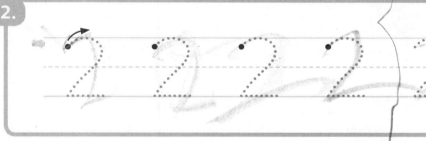

☐ Write 2.

3.

GK-2 Circles

☐ Count the ○.

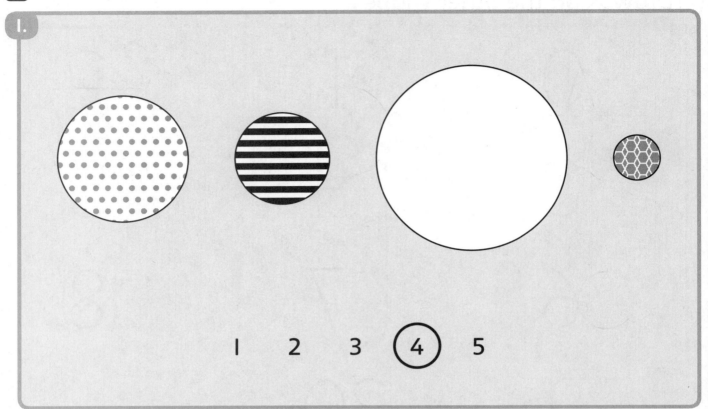

1   2   3   ④   5

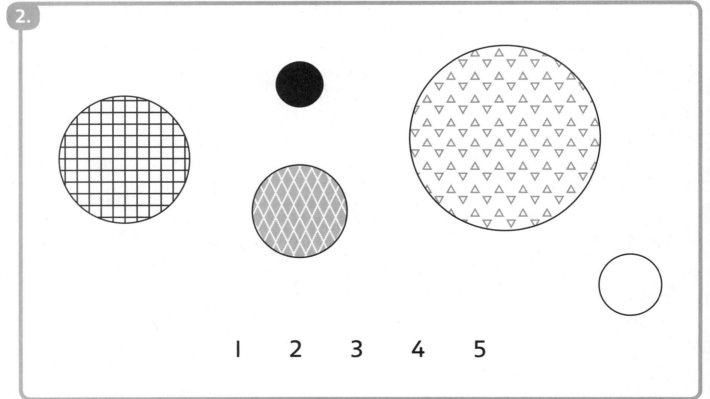

1   2   3   4   5

   Geometry K-2

☐ Colour the ○.
☐ Draw ✕ on the other shapes.

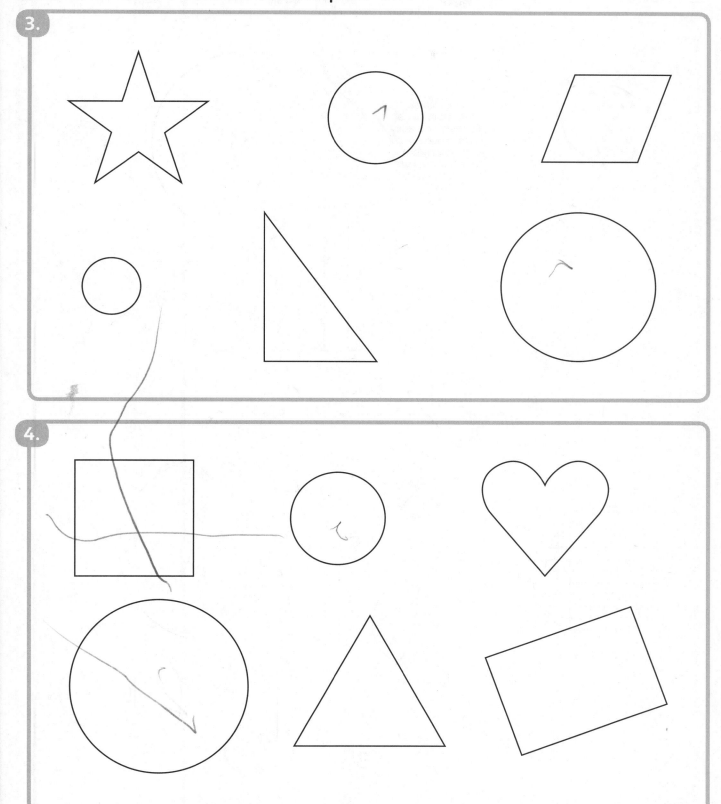

☐ Colour the ◯.
☐ Draw ✕ on the other shapes.

5.

6.

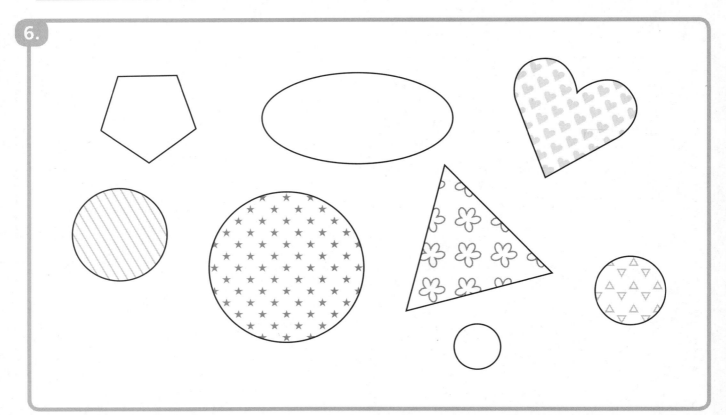

GK-3 Squares

☐ Count the ☐.

1.

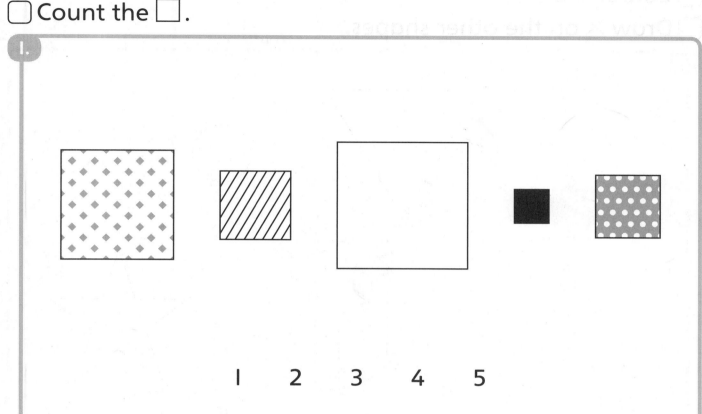

1   2   3   4   5

2.

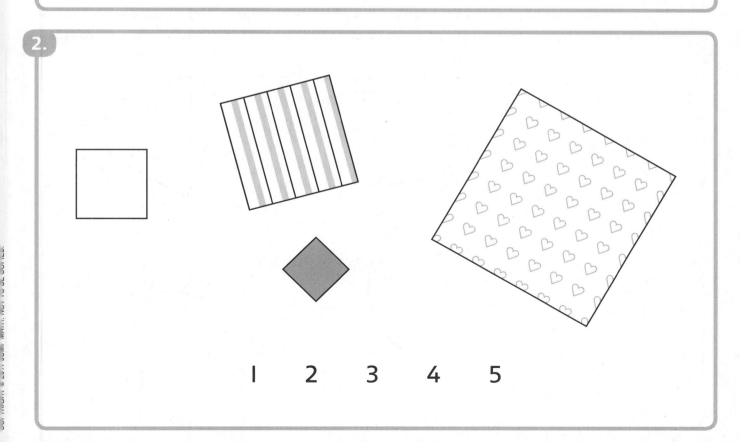

1   2   3   4   5

 Colour the ☐.
☐ Draw ✕ on the other shapes.

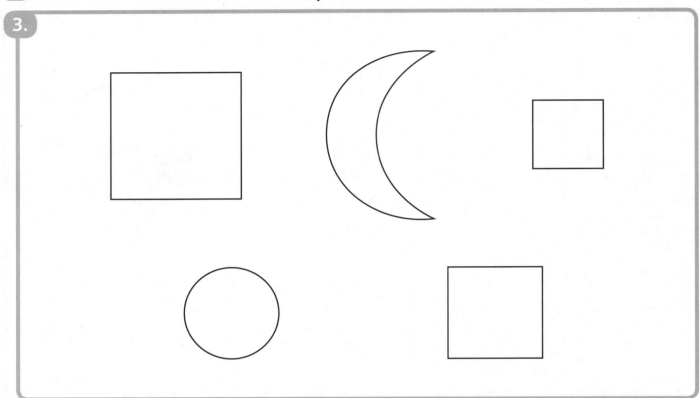

3.

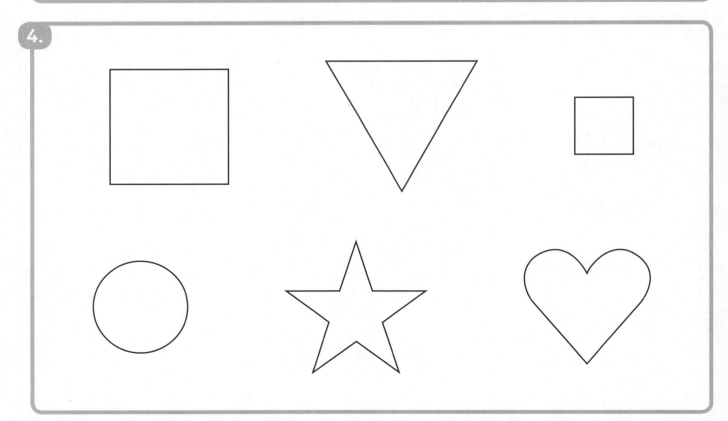

4.

☐ Colour the ☐.
☐ Draw ✕ on the other shapes.

5.

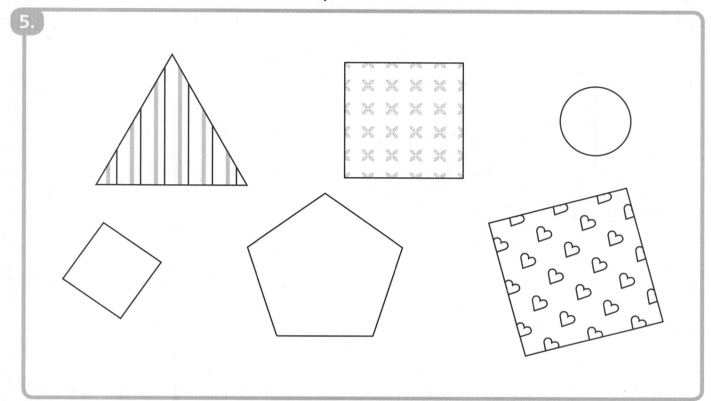

6.

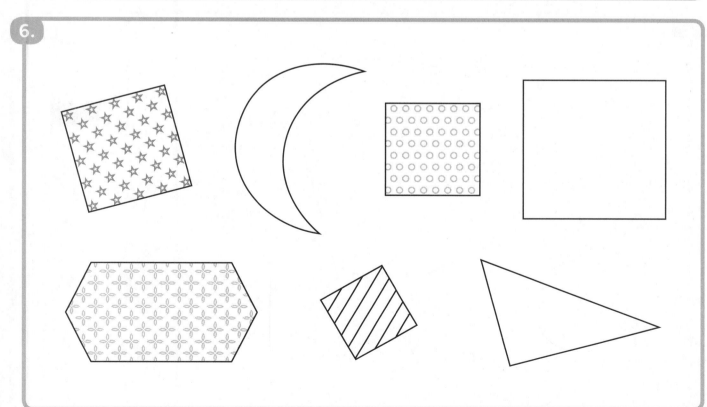

GK-4 Rectangles

Count the ▭.

1.

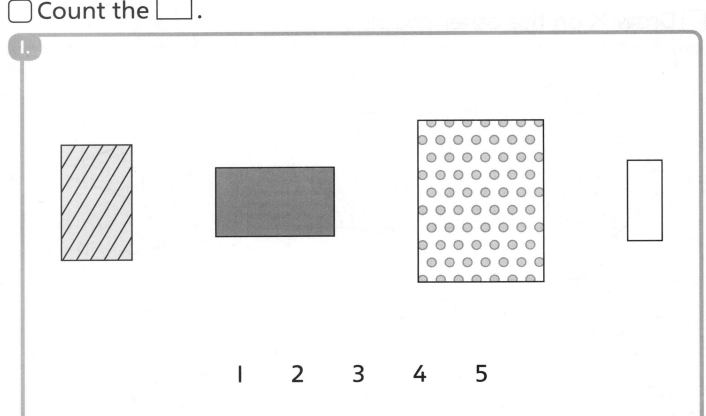

1   2   3   4   5

2.

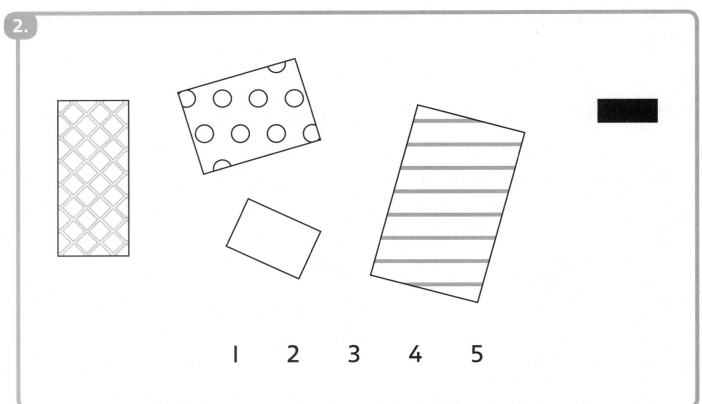

1   2   3   4   5

☐ Colour the ▭ .
☐ Draw ✕ on the other shapes.

3.

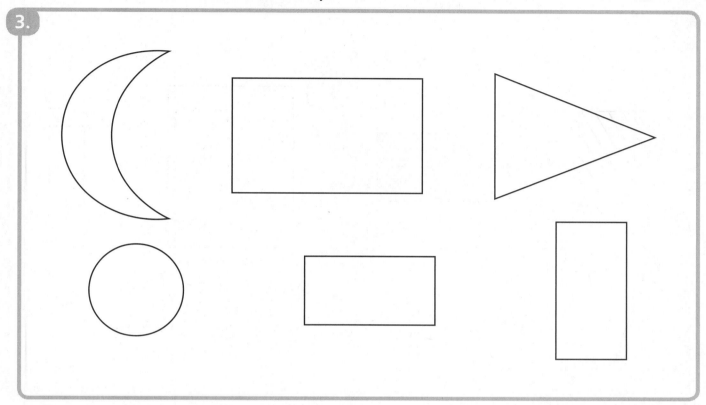

4.

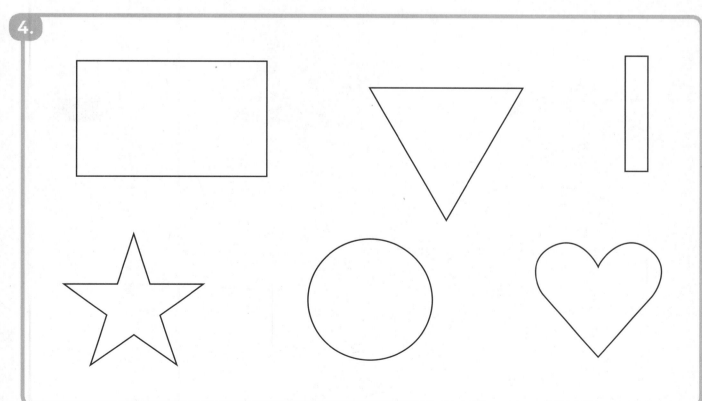

◻ Colour the ▢.
◻ Draw ✕ on the other shapes.

5.

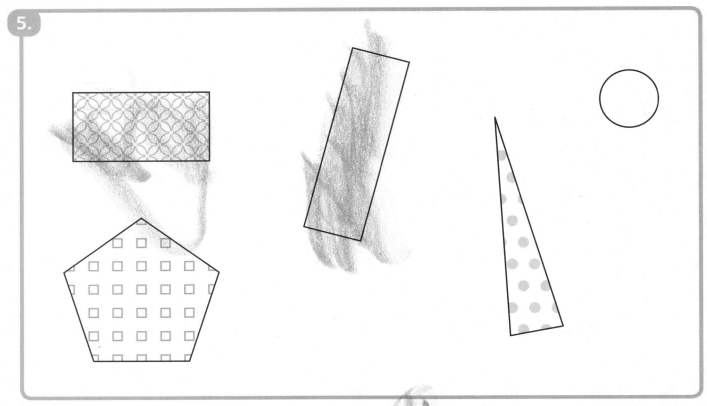

6.

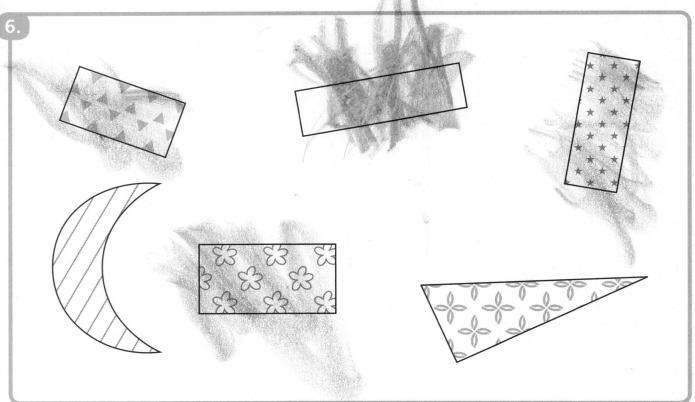

GK-5 Corners and Sides

⬜ Draw ● on each corner.

1.
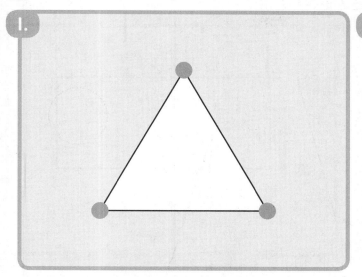

2.
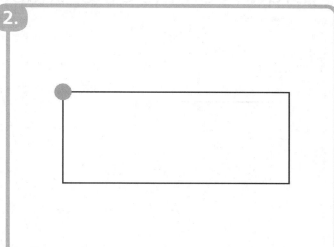

3.
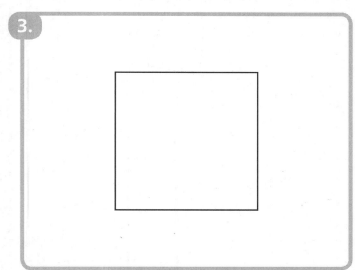

4.
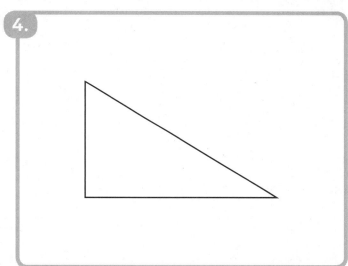

5.
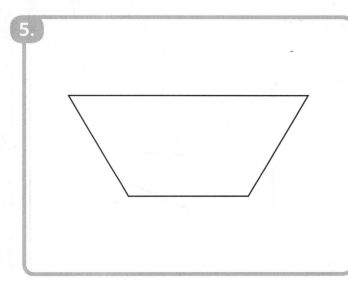

6.
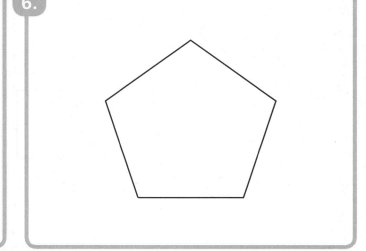

☐ Colour the sides.

7.

8.

9.

10.

11.

12.

GK-6 Counting Corners and Sides

☐ Draw ● on each corner.
☐ Count the corners.

1.

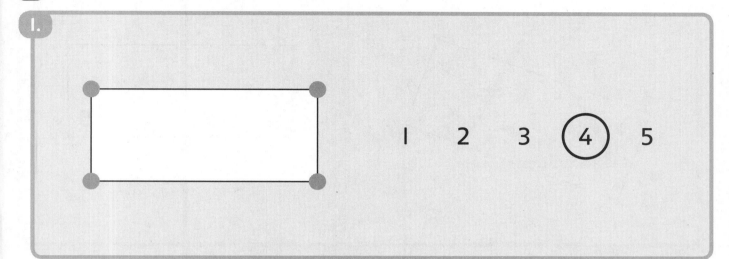

1   2   3   ④   5

2.

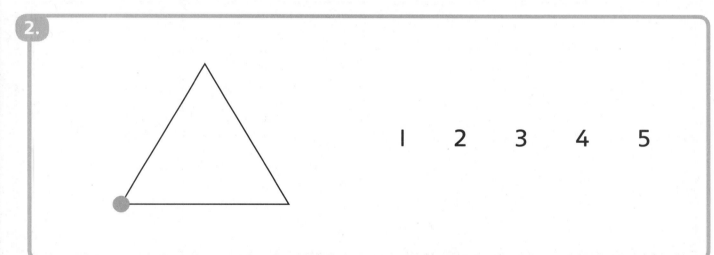

1   2   3   4   5

3.

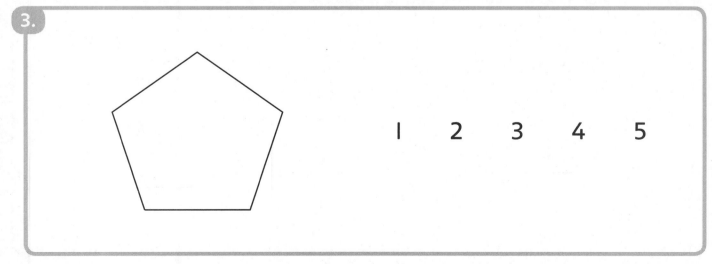

1   2   3   4   5

☐ Draw ● on each corner.
☐ Count the corners.

4.

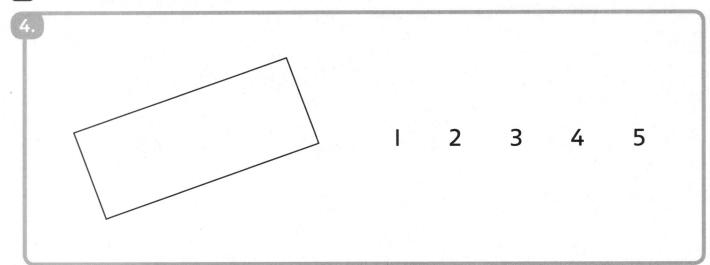

1   2   3   4   5

5.

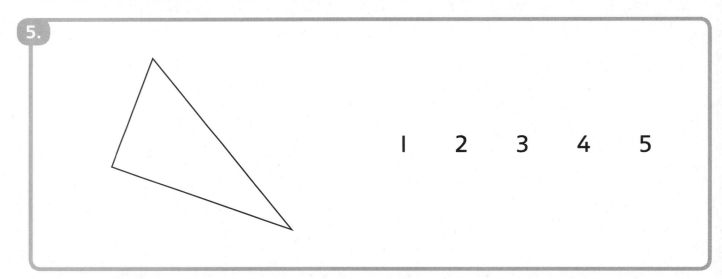

1   2   3   4   5

6.

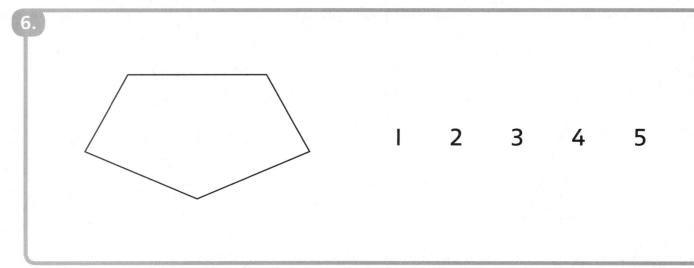

1   2   3   4   5

☐ Colour the sides.
☐ Count the sides.

7.

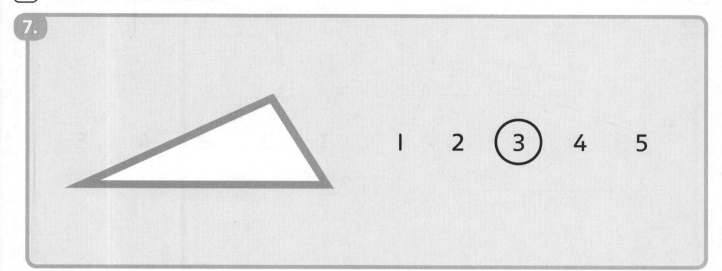

1   2   ③   4   5

8.

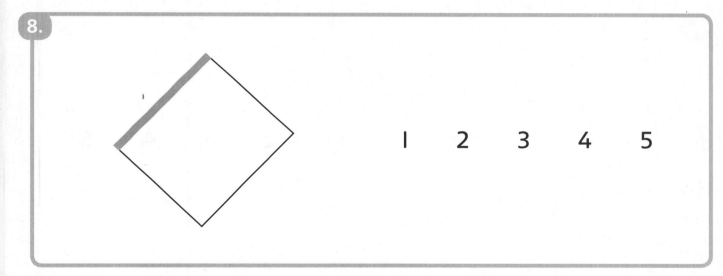

1   2   3   4   5

9.

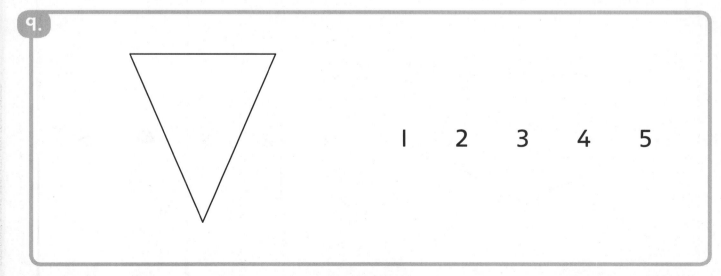

1   2   3   4   5

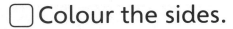 Colour the sides.
☐ Count the sides.

10.

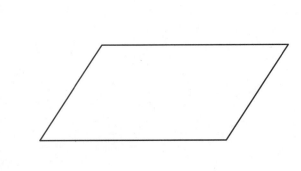

1   2   3   4   5

11.

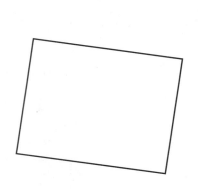

1   2   3   4   5

12.

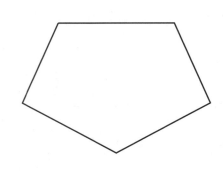

1   2   3   4   5

GK-7 More Squares and Rectangles

 Count the .

I.

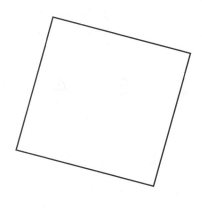
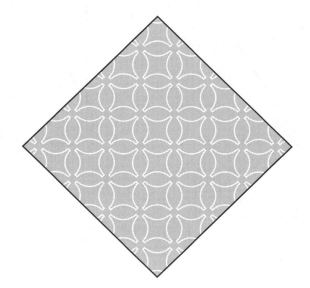

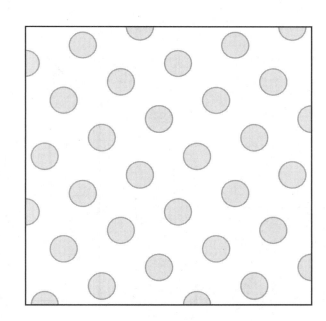

1   2   3   4   5

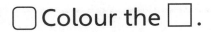 Colour the ▢.
◻ Draw ✕ on the other shapes.

2.
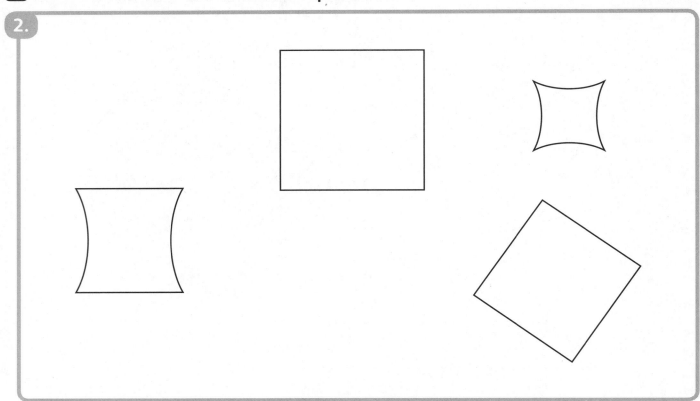

3.
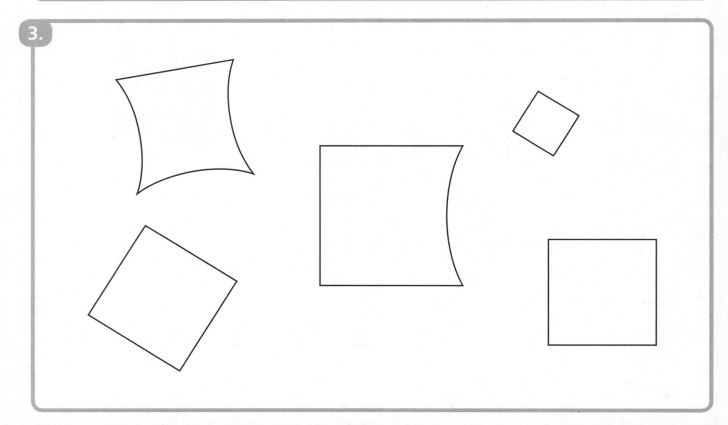

☐ Count the ☐ .

4.

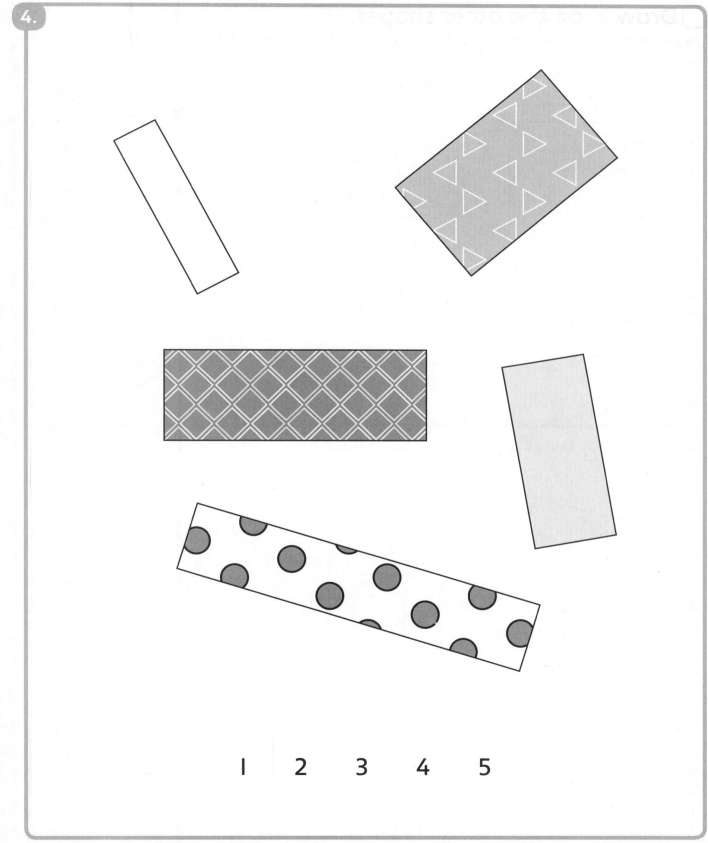

1 2 3 4 5

Colour the ▢.

Draw ✕ on the other shapes.

5.

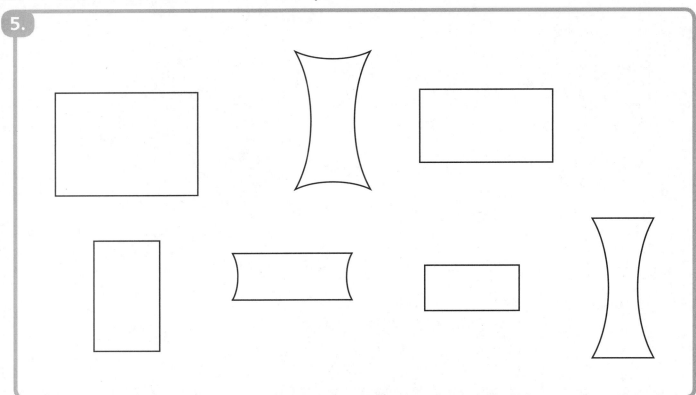

6.

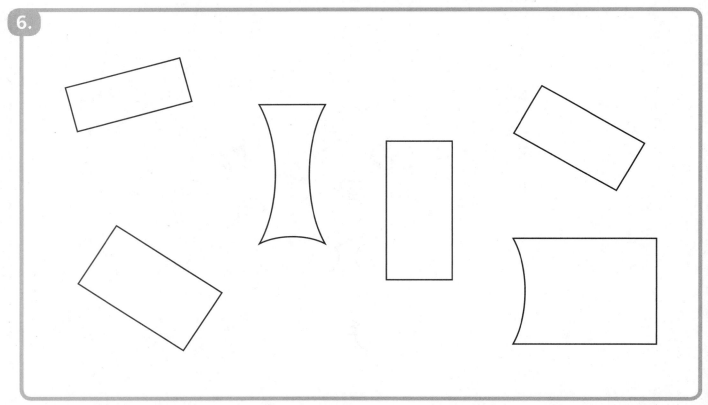

GK-8 Triangles

☐ Count the △.

1.

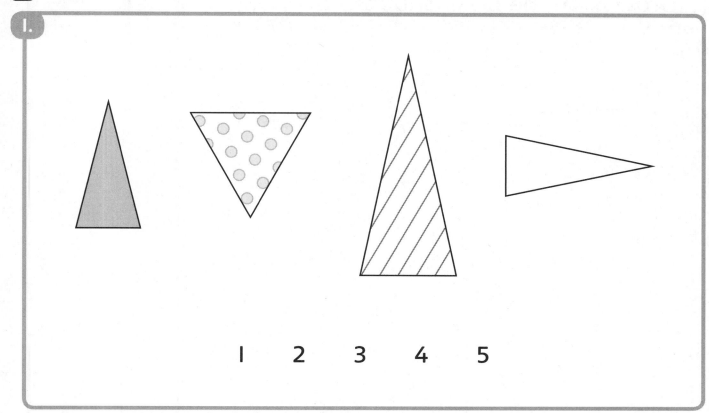

1   2   3   4   5

2.

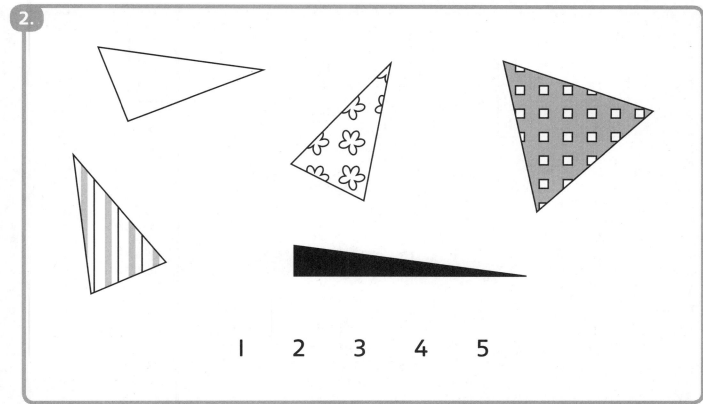

1   2   3   4   5

☐ Colour the △.
☐ Draw ✕ on the other shapes.

3.

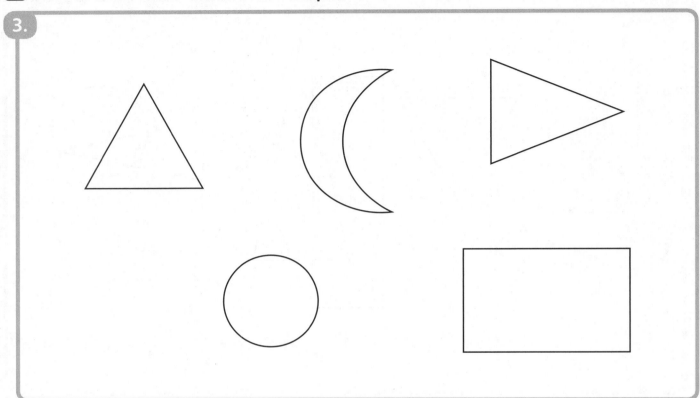

4.

☐ Colour the △.
☐ Draw ✕ on the other shapes.

5.

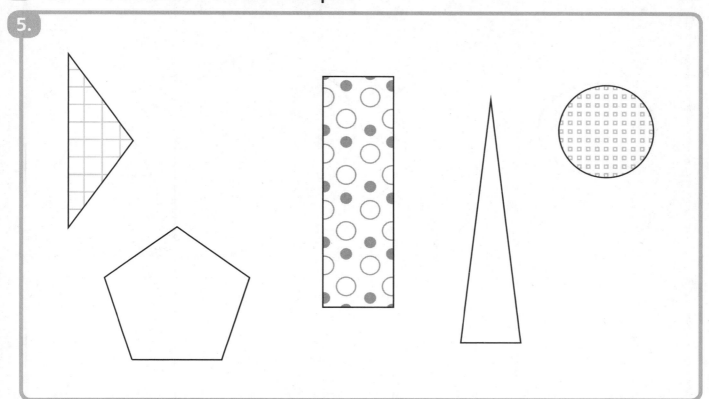

6.

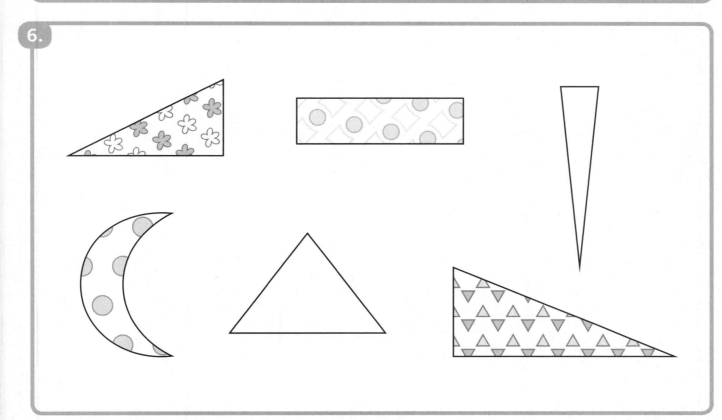

GK-9 Describing and Comparing Shapes

☐ Circle the shapes that are the **same**.

1.

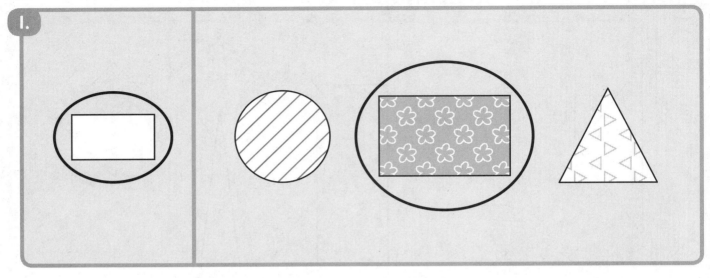

2.

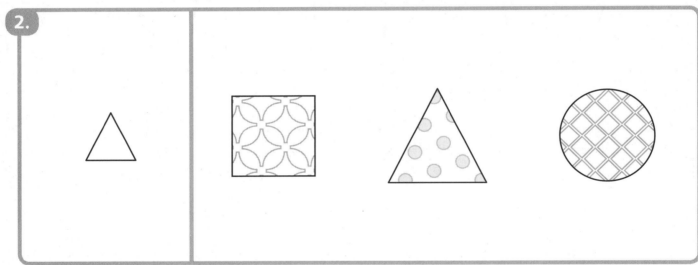

3.

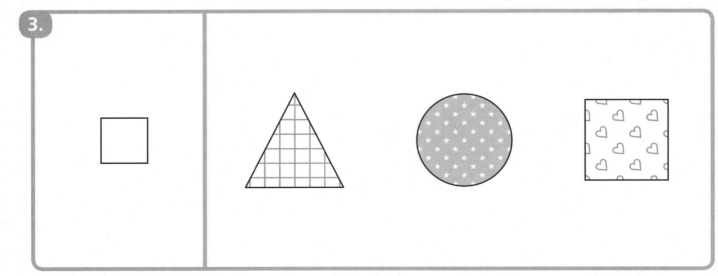

☐ Circle the shapes that are the same.

4.

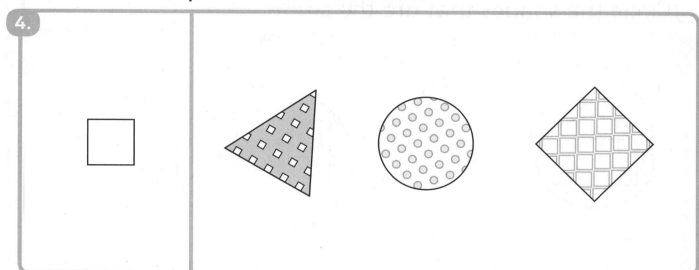

5.

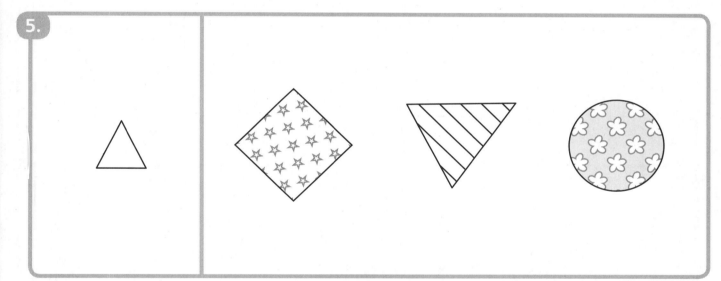

6.

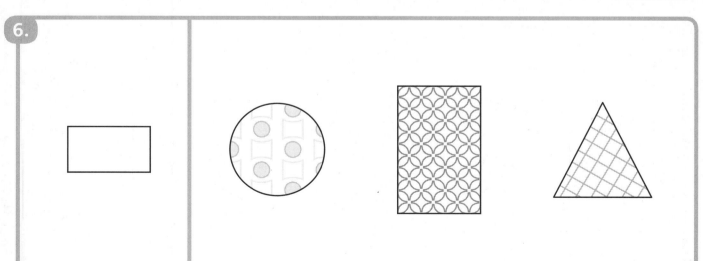

GK-10 Above

☐ Circle the shape that is **above**.

1.
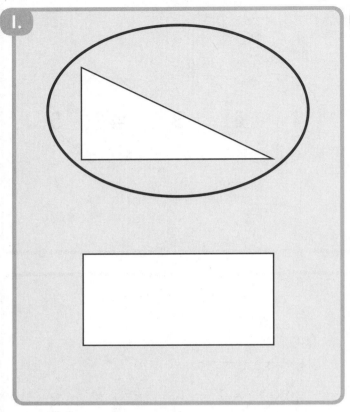

2.
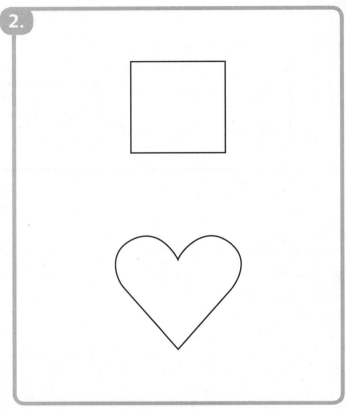

3.
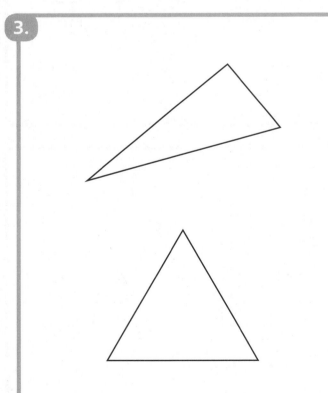

4.
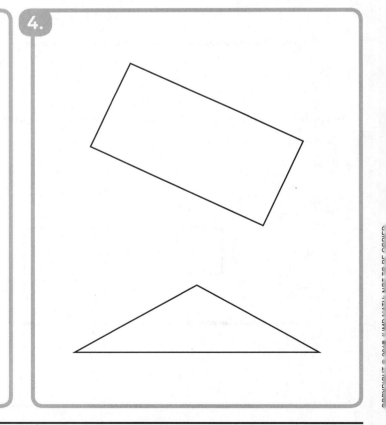

How many shapes are above the line?

5.

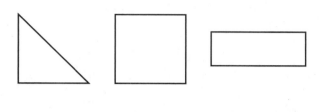

1   2   3   4   5

6.

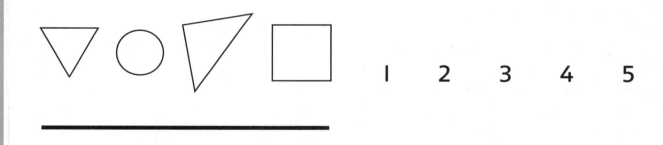

1   2   3   4   5

7.

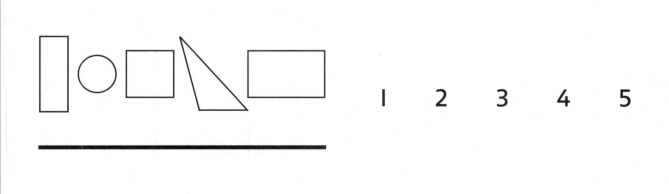

1   2   3   4   5

How many shapes are above the line?

8.

1   2   3   4   5

9.

1   2   3   4   5

10.

1   2   3   4   5

GK-11 Below

☐ Circle the shape that is **below**.

1.

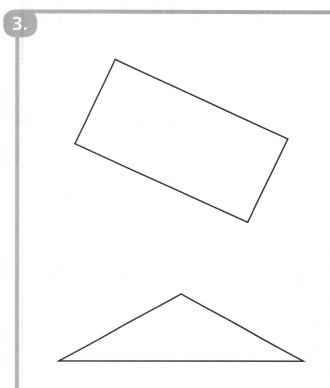

2.

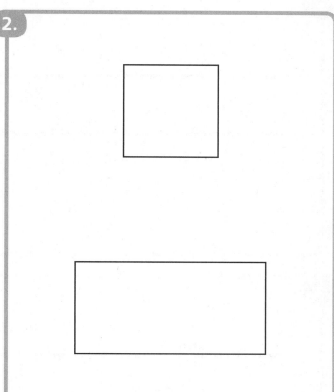

3.

4.

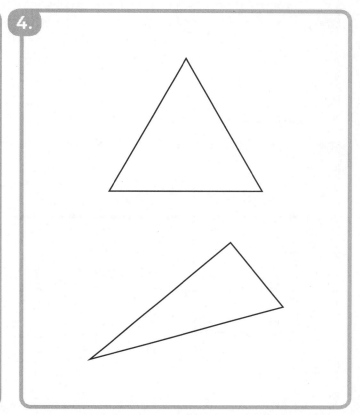

☐ How many shapes are below the line?

5.

$1 \quad 2 \quad 3 \quad 4 \quad 5$

6.

$1 \quad 2 \quad 3 \quad 4 \quad 5$

7.

$1 \quad 2 \quad 3 \quad 4 \quad 5$

☐ How many shapes are below the line?

8.

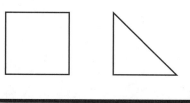

1   2   3   4   5

9.

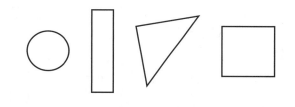

1   2   3   4   5

10.

1   2   3   4   5

GK-12 Near, Far, and Beside

☐ Draw ✕ on the shape **beside** the ◯.

1.

2.

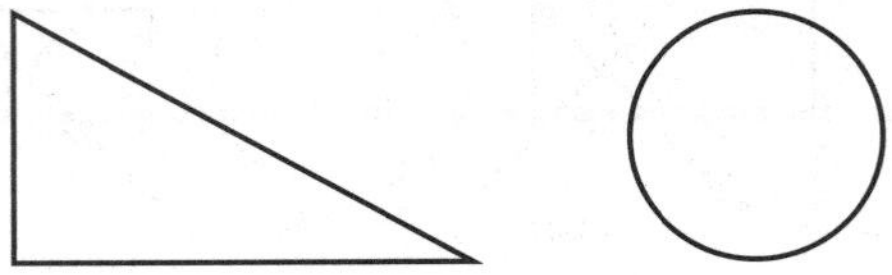

3.

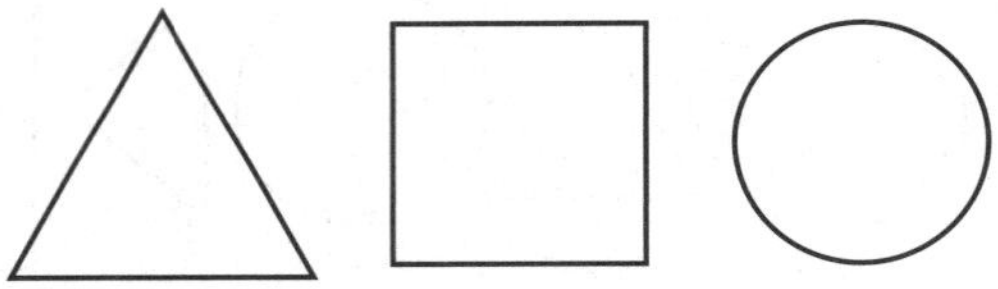

4.

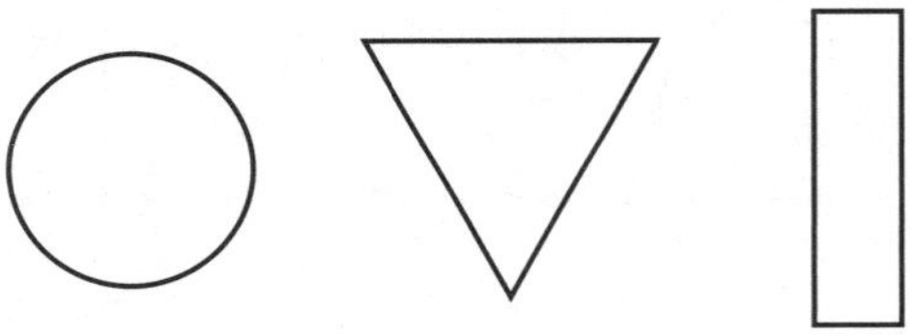

5.

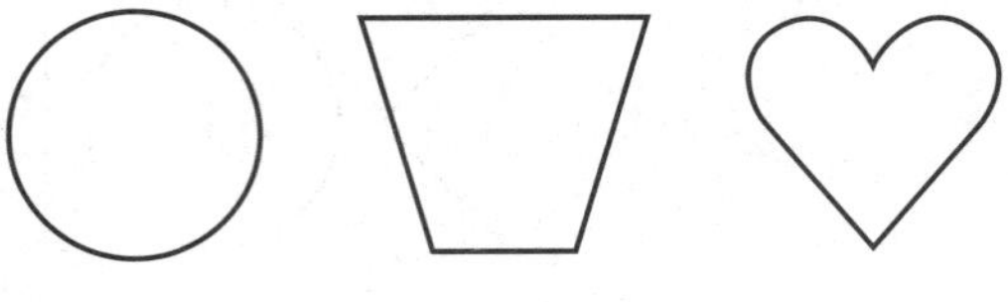

6.

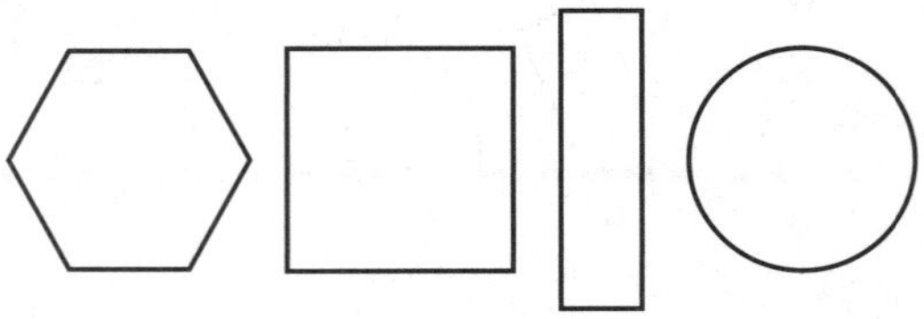

☐ Draw ✕ on the shapes beside the ◯.

7.

8.

9.

10.

11.

12.
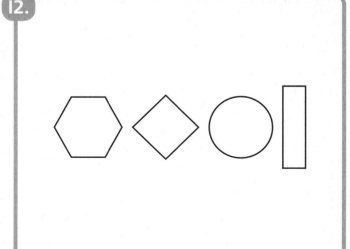

GK-13 Combining Shapes

Use **2** pattern blocks to cover the shape.

1.

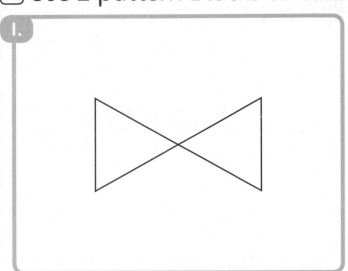

2.

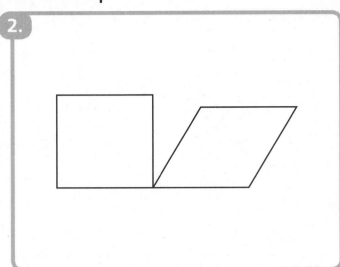

3.

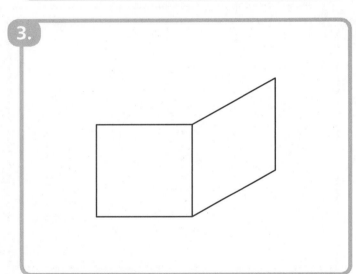

4.

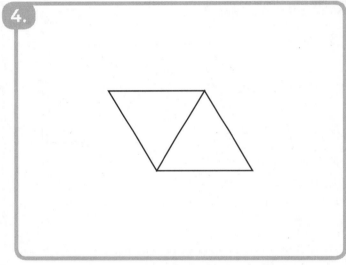

5.

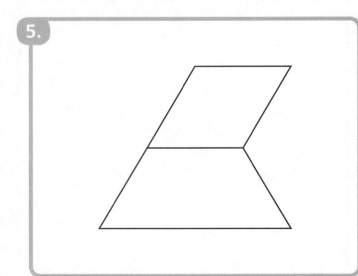

6.

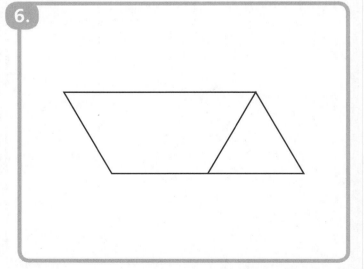

Geometry K-13

Use pattern blocks to cover the shape.

7.

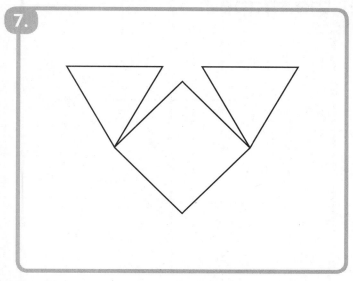

8.

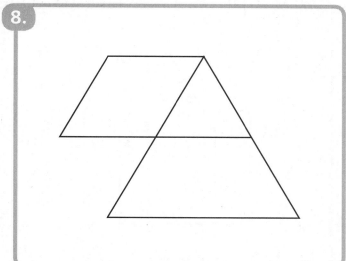

9.

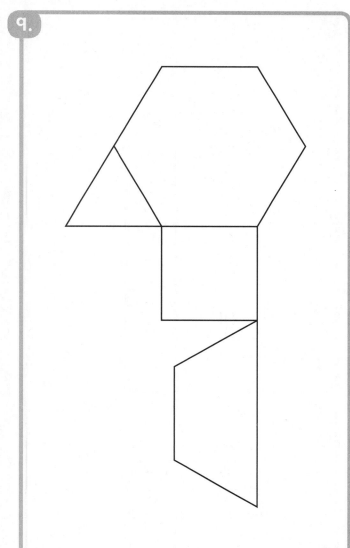

10.

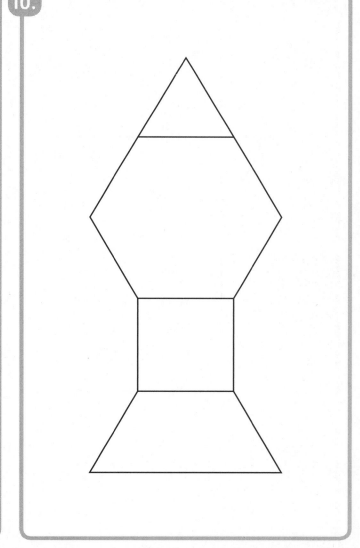

☐ Use pattern blocks to cover the shape.

11.

12.

13.

14.

GK-14 Decomposing Flat Shapes

☐ Trace the lines to make smaller shapes.

1.
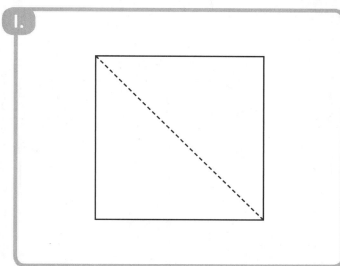

2.
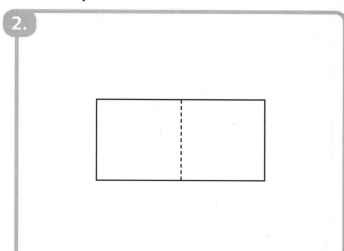

3.
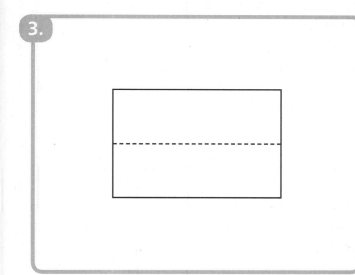

4.
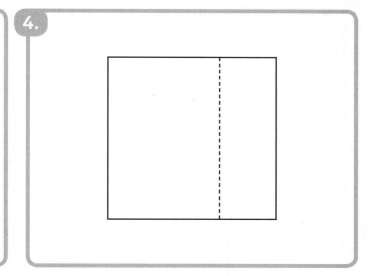

5.
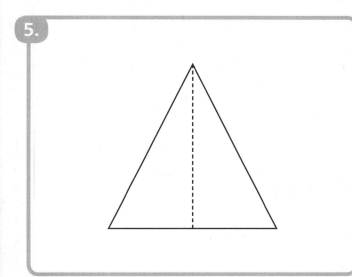

6.
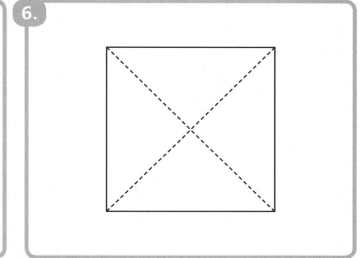

Colour the ☐.

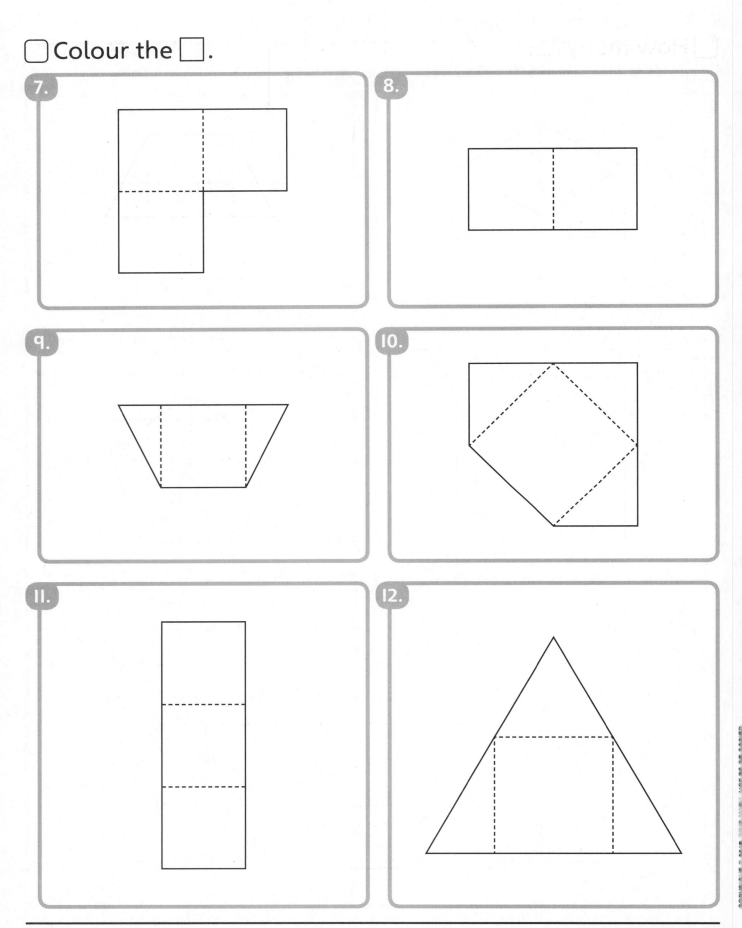

7.

8.

9.

10.

11.

12.

☐ How many △?

13.

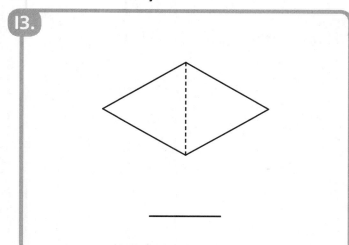

_____

14.

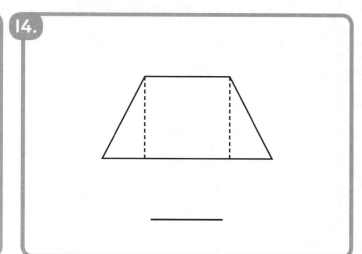

_____

15.

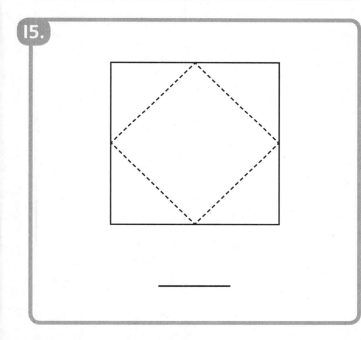

_____

16.

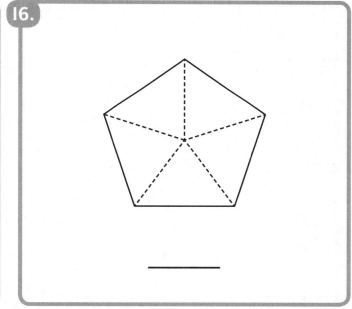

_____

17.

_____

GK-15 Symmetry in Shapes

Zack cuts along the dotted lines.
☐ Circle the pictures that make the same kinds of shapes.

1.

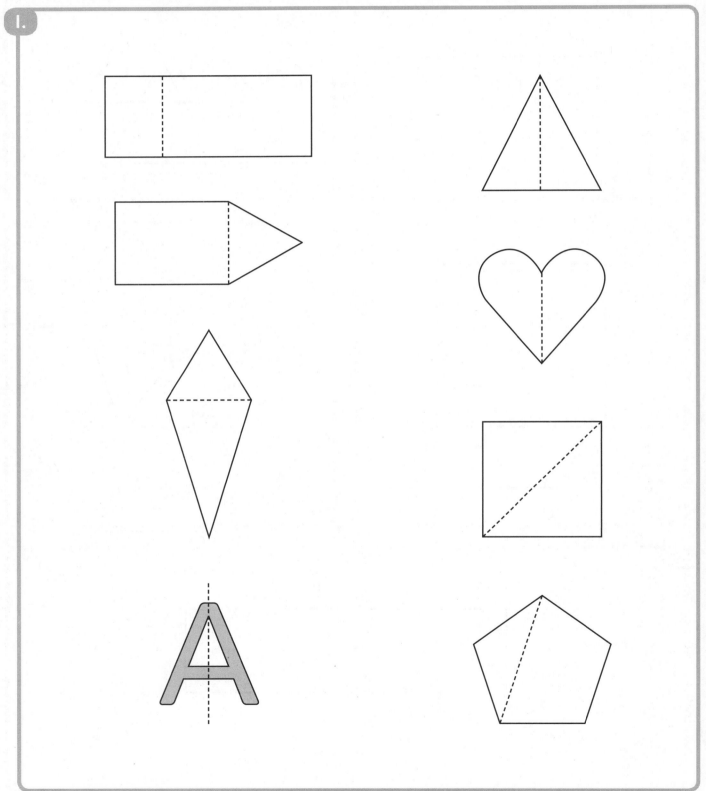

NAME _____

Zack cuts along the dotted lines.
☐ Circle if the 2 shapes match exactly.

2.

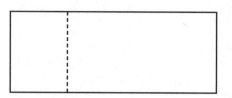

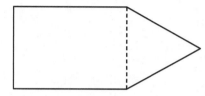

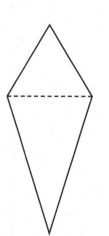

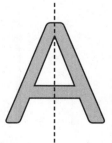

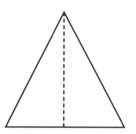

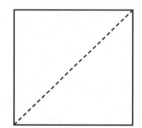

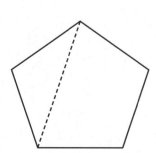

PAK-I Counting to 40

☐ Trace.

1.

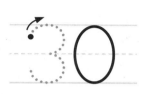 0    1    2

 3    4    5

 6    7    8

 9   40

2.

☐ Write 3.

3.

PAK-2 Ordinal Numbers

☐ Circle the 1st or 2nd.

1.

2nd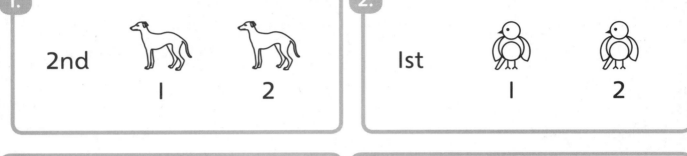

1   2

2.

1st

1   2

3.

1st

1   2

4.

2nd

1   2

5.

1st

1   2

6.

2nd

1   2

7.

2nd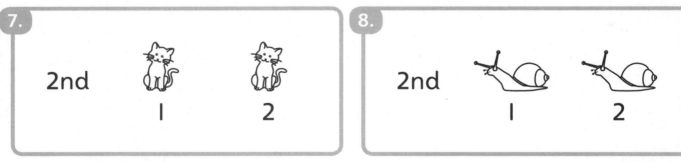

1   2

8.

2nd

1   2

9.

1st

1   2

10.

1st

1   2

    Patterns and Algebra K-2

☐ Circle the 3rd, 4th, or 5th.

11.

3rd

1   2   3   4   5

12.

5th

1   2   3   4   5

13.

4th

1   2   3   4   5

14.

3rd

1   2   3   4   5

15.

5th

1   2   3   4   5

☐ Circle the 1st, 2nd, 3rd, 4th, or 5th.

16. 2nd
1   2   3   4   5

17. 4th
1   2   3   4   5

18. 3rd
1   2   3   4   5

19. 5th
1   2   3   4   5

20. 1st
1   2   3   4   5

PAK-3 Patterns in Motion

☐ Circle the action that comes next.

1.

2.

3.

Circle the action that comes next.

4.

5.

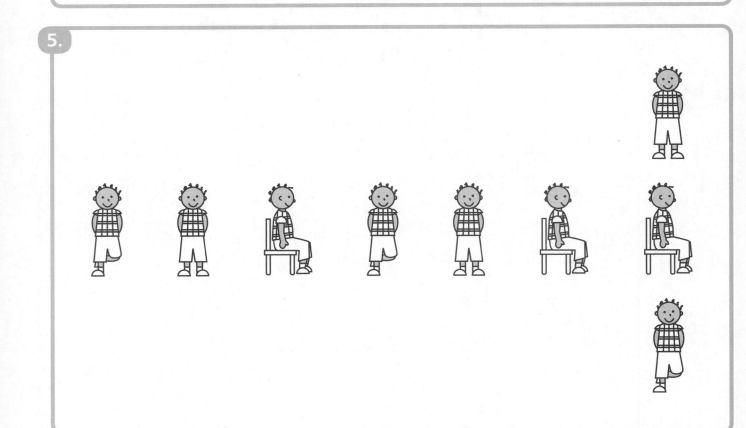

☐ Circle the action that comes next.

6.

7.

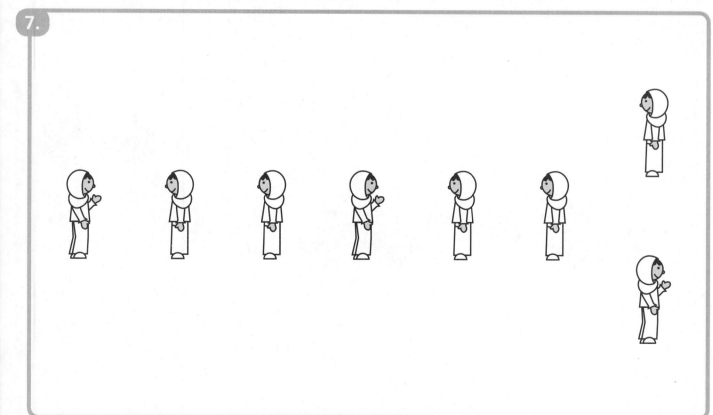

PAK-4 Patterns with Objects

☐ Circle the object that comes next.

1.

2.

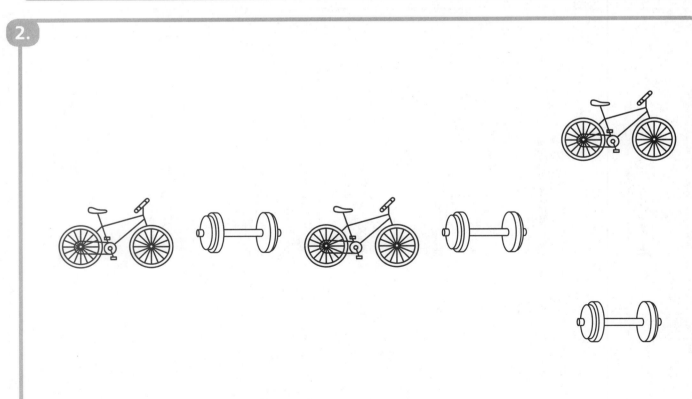

☐ Circle the object that comes next.

3.

4.

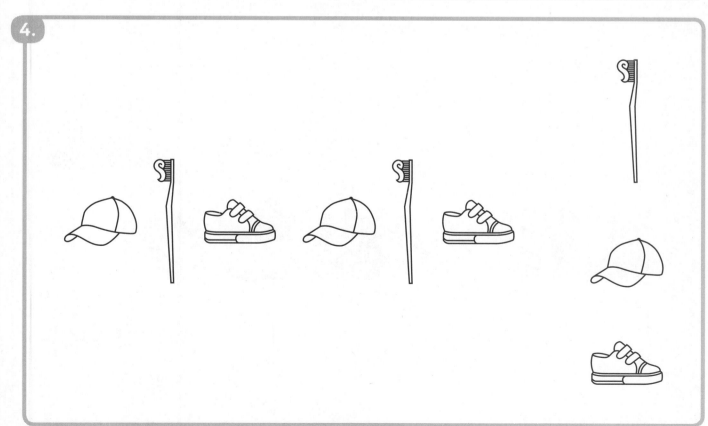

☐ Circle the object that comes next.

5.

6.

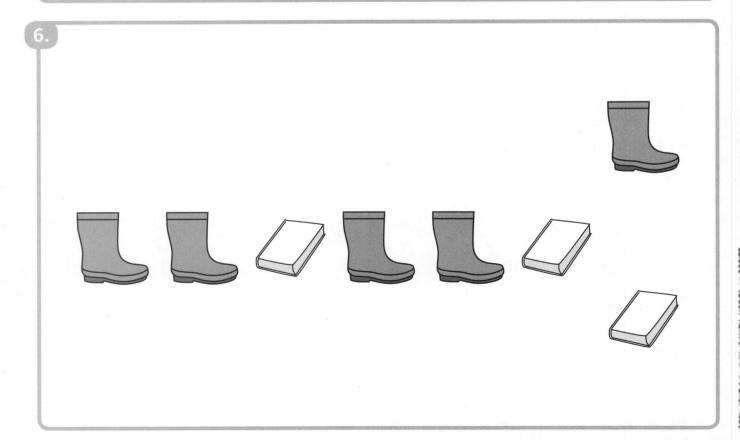

    Patterns and Algebra K-4

PAK-5 Patterns with Pictures

☐ Underline every core.

1.

2.

3.

4.

☐ Underline every core.

5.

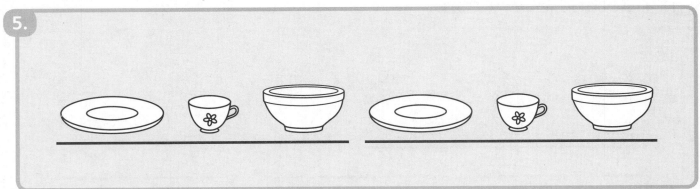

6.

7.

8.

Patterns and Algebra K-5

Underline every core.

9.

10.

11.

12.

☐ Underline every core.

13.

14.

15.

16.

PAK-6 Creating Patterns

☐ Colour the core with 2 colours.
☐ Repeat the pattern.
☐ Underline every core.

1.

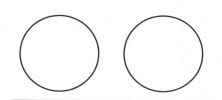

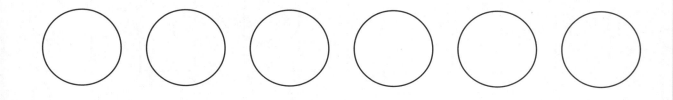

2.

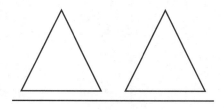

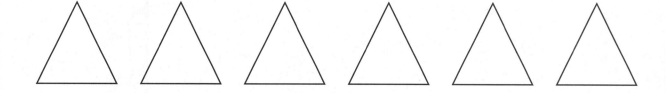

☐ Colour the core with 3 colours.
☐ Repeat the pattern.
☐ Underline every core.

3.

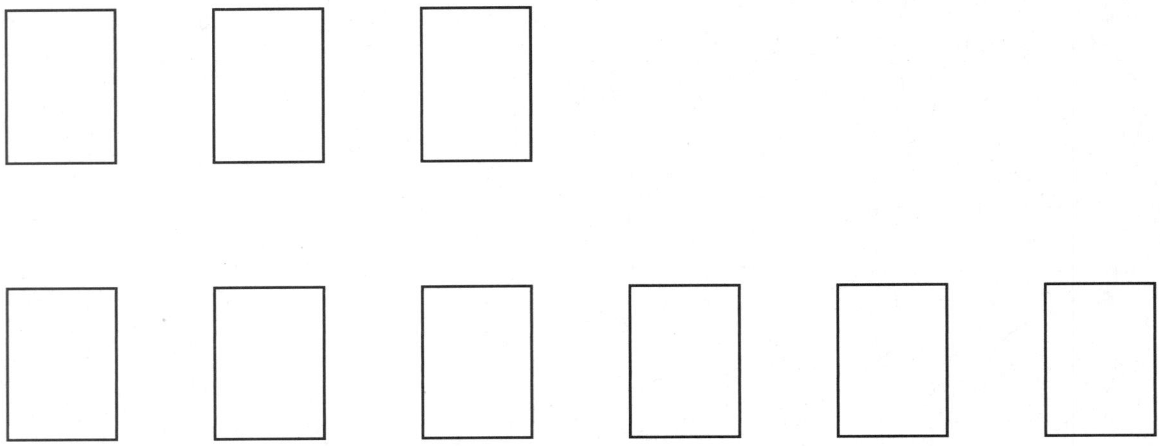

4.

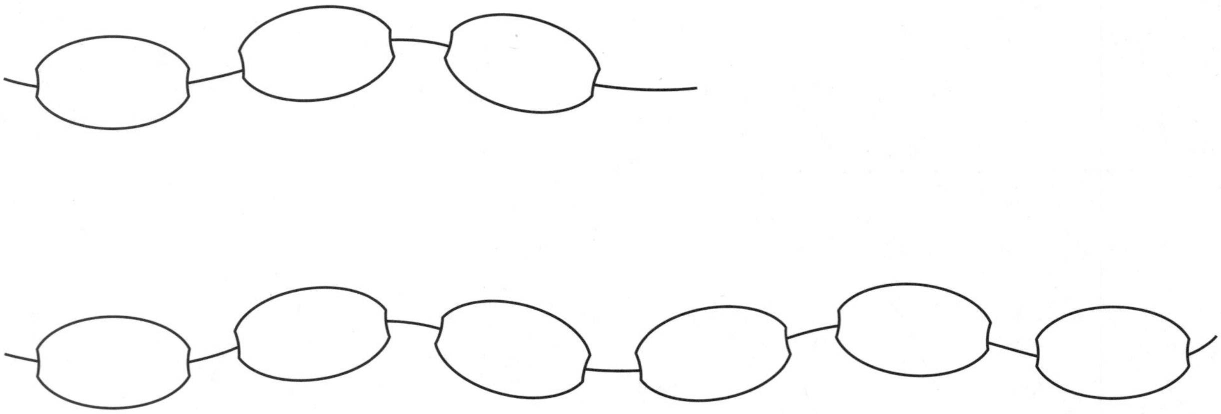

NSK-25 Counting to 50

☐ Trace.

1.

2.

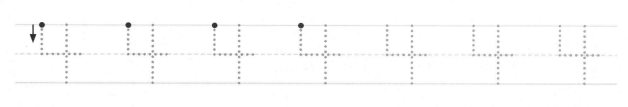

☐ Write 4.

3.

NSK-26 Counting 6 and 7

How many?

☐ Count. Circle the number.

1.

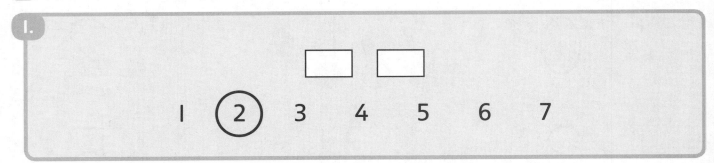

1   ② 3   4   5   6   7

2.

○ ○ ○ ○ ○ ○

1   2   3   4   5   6   7

3.

1   2   3   4   5   6   7

4.

1   2   3   4   5   6   7

How many?

☐ Count. Circle the number.

5.

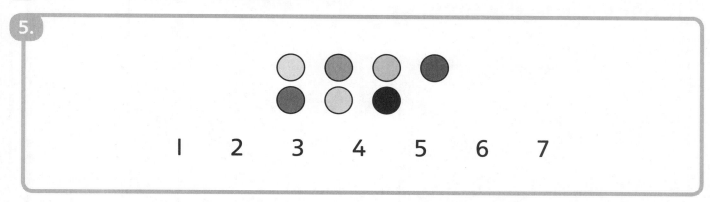

1	2	3	4	5	6	7

6.

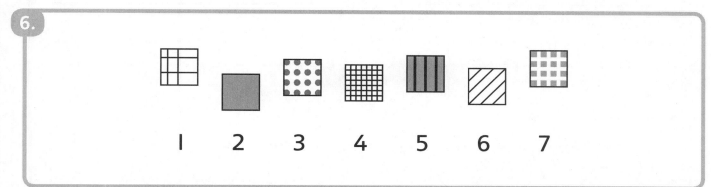

1	2	3	4	5	6	7

7.

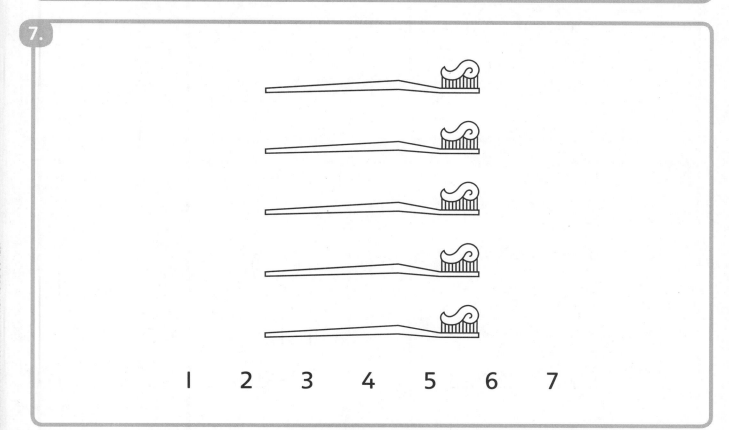

1	2	3	4	5	6	7

◻ Show counting out.

8.

2

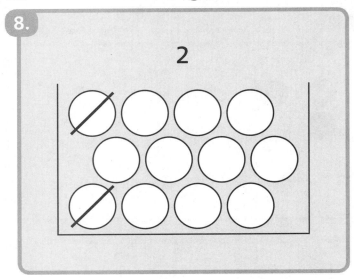

9.

5

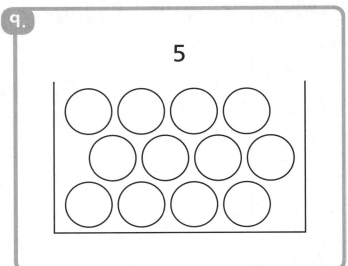

10.

3

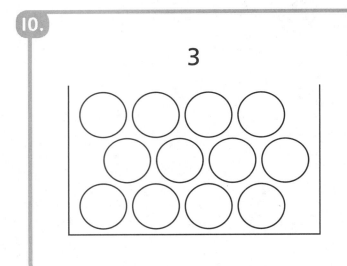

11.

6

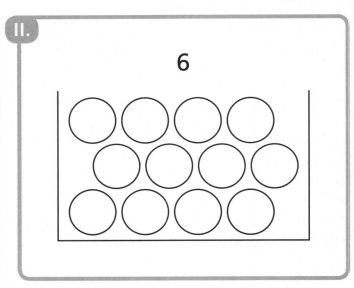

12.

7

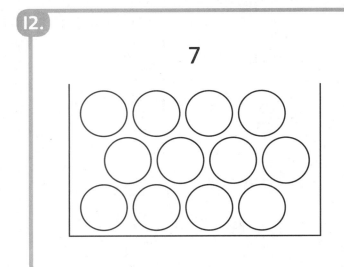

13.

4

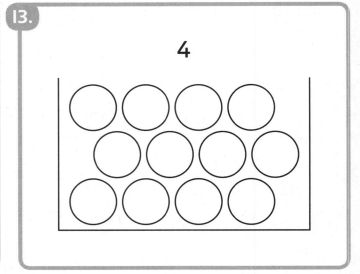

NSK-27 The Numbers 6 and 7

 Match by drawing lines.

1.
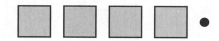   • 4

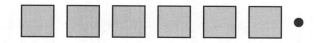   • 6

2.
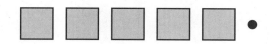   • 5

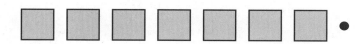   • 7

3.
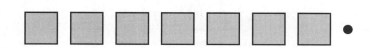   • 6

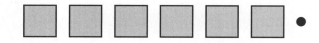   • 7

4.
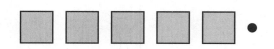   • 5

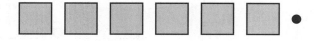   • 6

Match by drawing lines.

5.

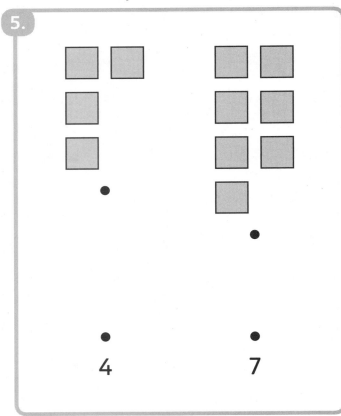

4   7

6.

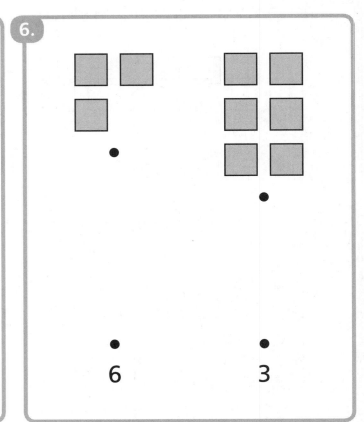

6   3

7.

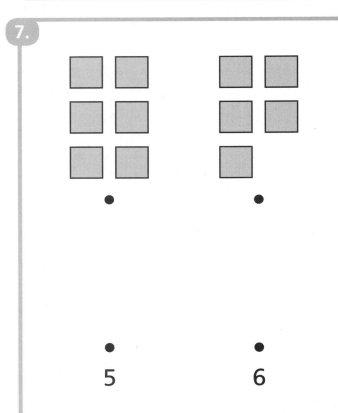

5   6

8.

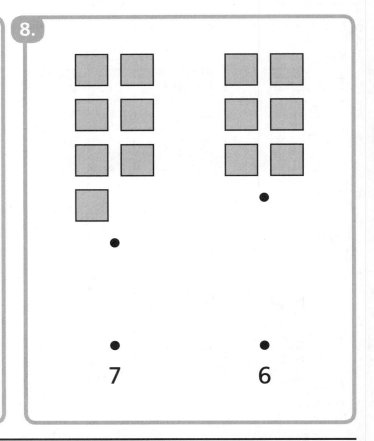

7   6

☐ Match by drawing lines.

9.

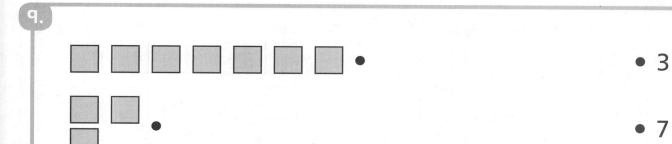

          • 3

          • 7

10.

          • 4

          • 5

11.

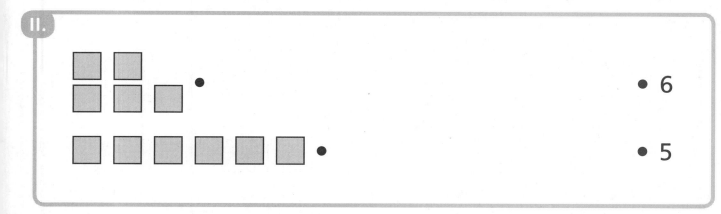

          • 6

          • 5

12.

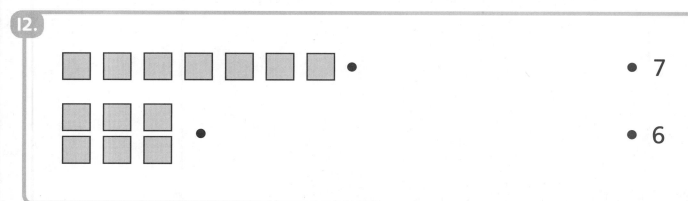

          • 7

          • 6

☐ Trace.

1.

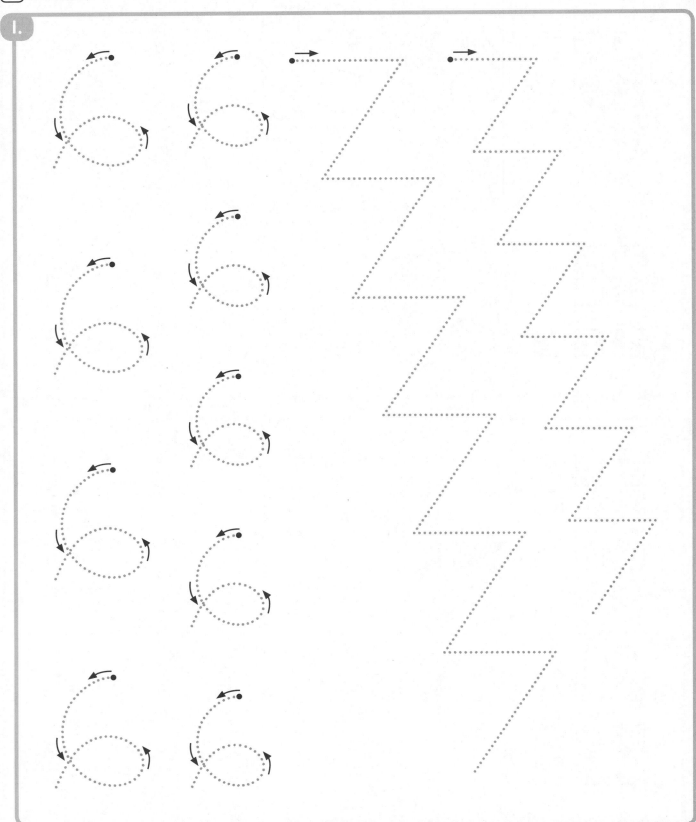

☐ Trace.

2.

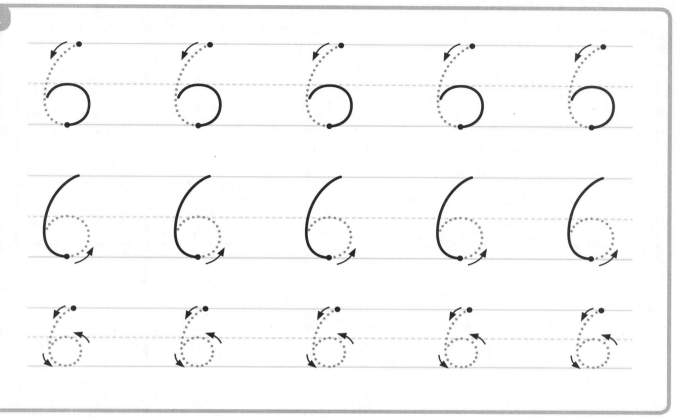

3.

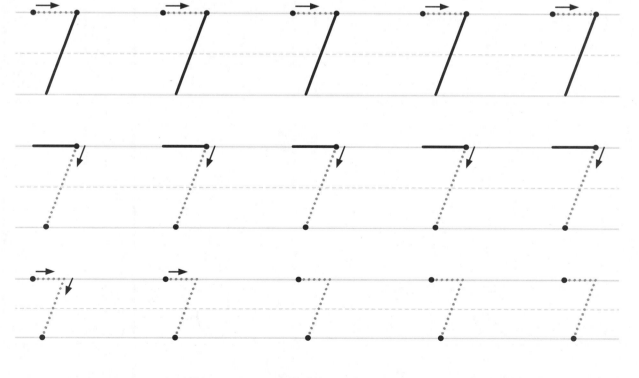

☐ Show counting out.

1.
4

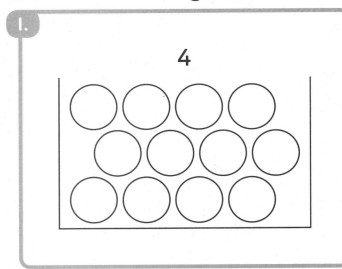

2.
6

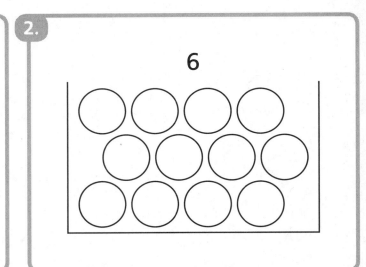

3.
9

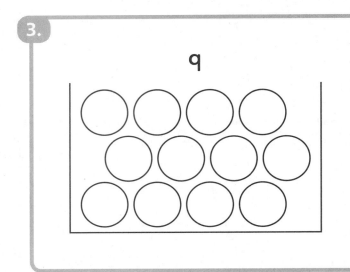

4.
8

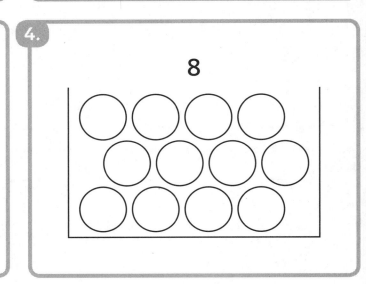

5.
7

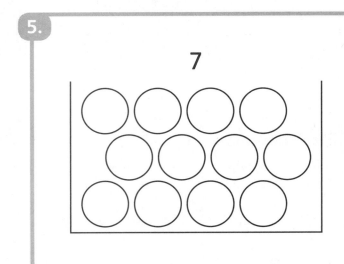

6.
5

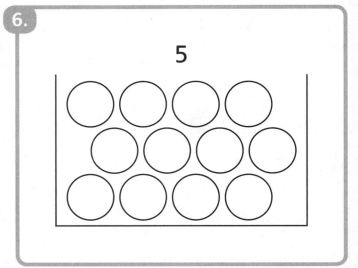

☐ Use 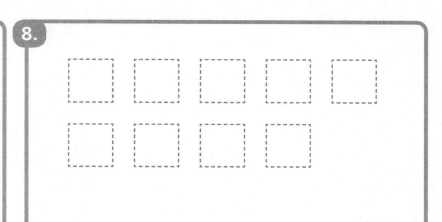.
☐ Move and count each ▢.
☐ Circle the number.

7.

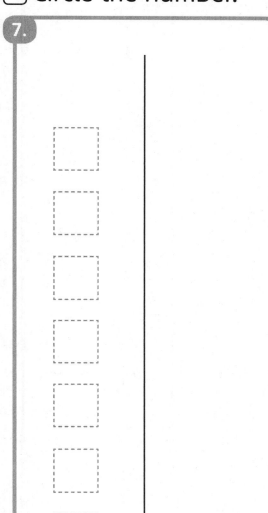

8   9

8.

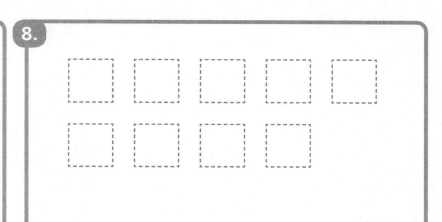

8   9

☐ Use ■.
☐ Move and count each ■.
☐ Circle the number.

9.

8   q

10.

8   q

NSK-30 The Numbers 8 and 9

☐ Match by drawing lines.

1.

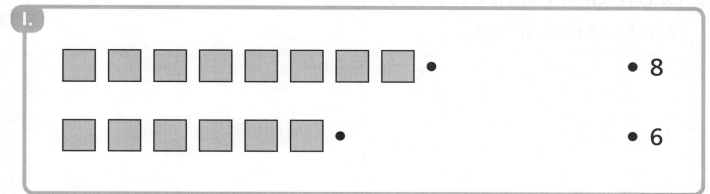

8

6

2.

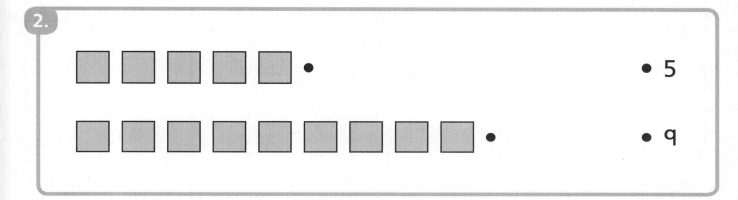

5

q

3.

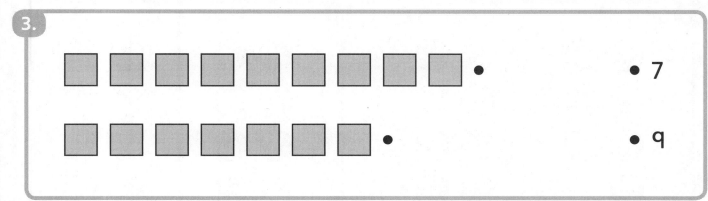

7

q

4.

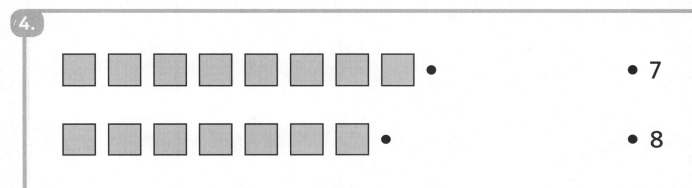

7

8

Match by drawing lines.

5.

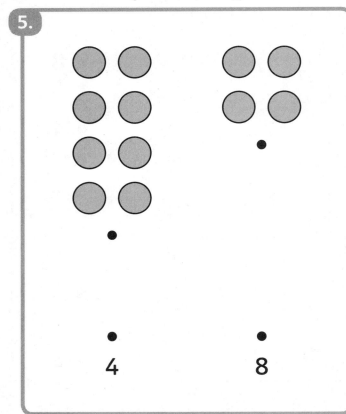

4   8

6.

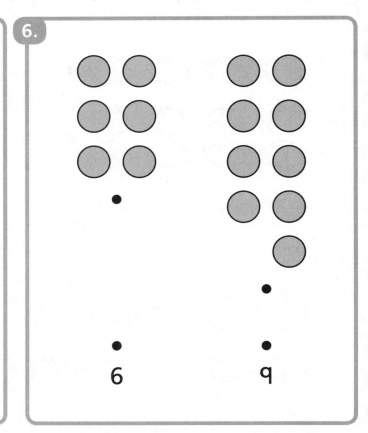

6   q

7.

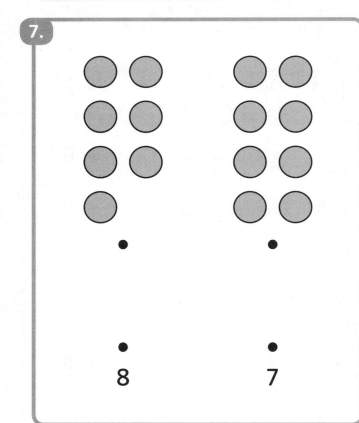

8   7

8.

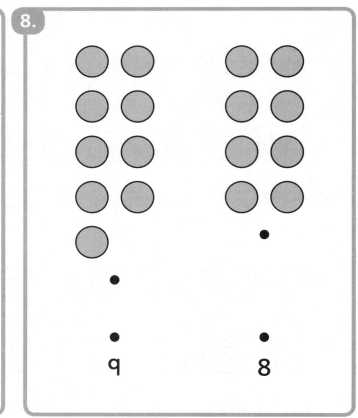

q   8

☐ BONUS: Match by drawing lines.

9.

•   • 8

•   • 4

10.

•   • 9

•   • 5

11.

•   • 8

•   • 9

12.

•   • 6

•   • 9

☐ Trace.

I.

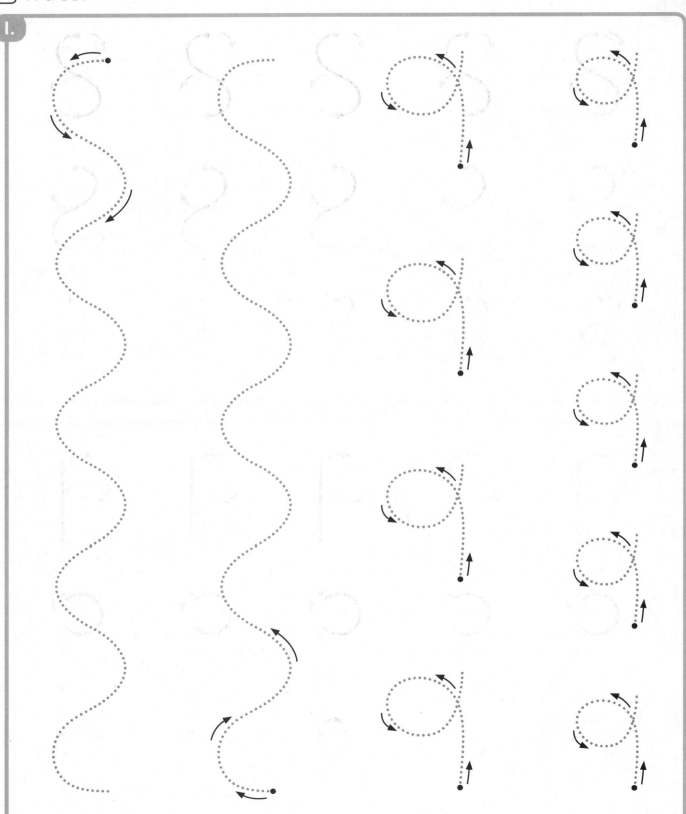

☐ Trace.

2.

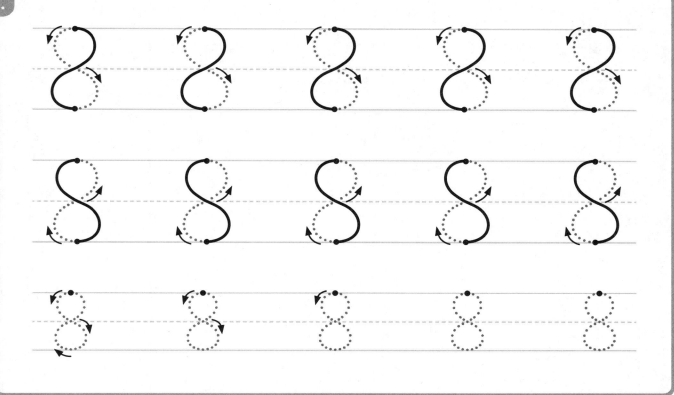

3.

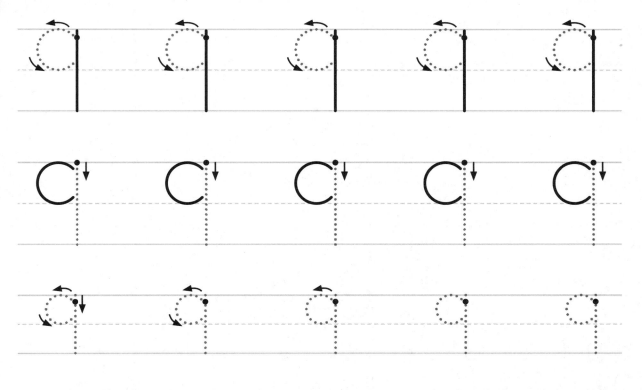

NSK-32 Counting 10

How many?
☐ Count. Circle the number.

1.

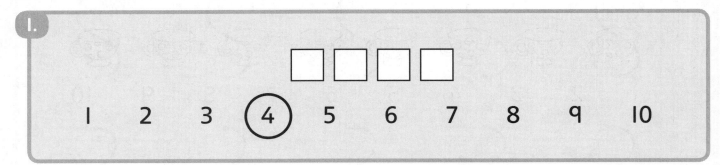

1 2 3 ④ 5 6 7 8 9 10

2.

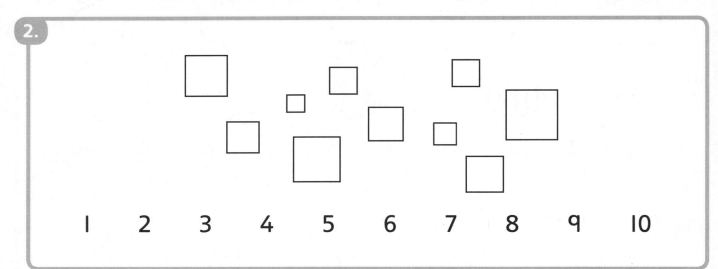

1   2   3   4   5   6   7   8   9   10

3.

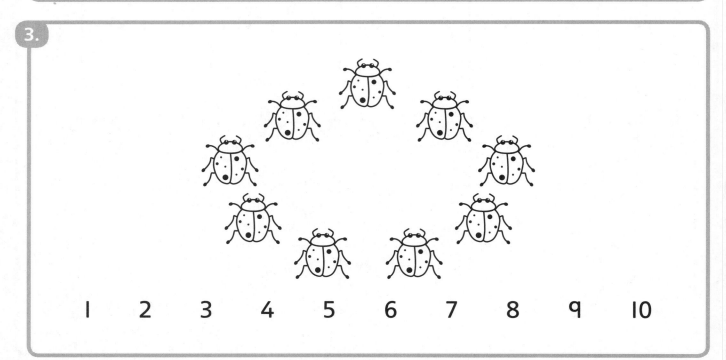

1   2   3   4   5   6   7   8   9   10

How many?
☐ Count. Circle the number.

4.

1   2   3   4   5   6   7   8   9   10

5.

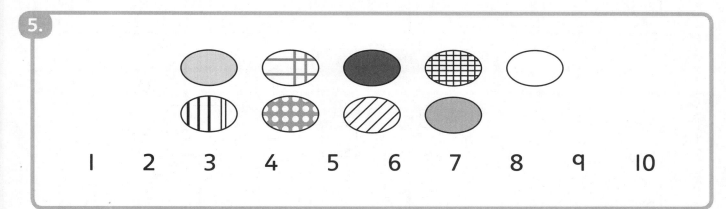

1   2   3   4   5   6   7   8   9   10

6.

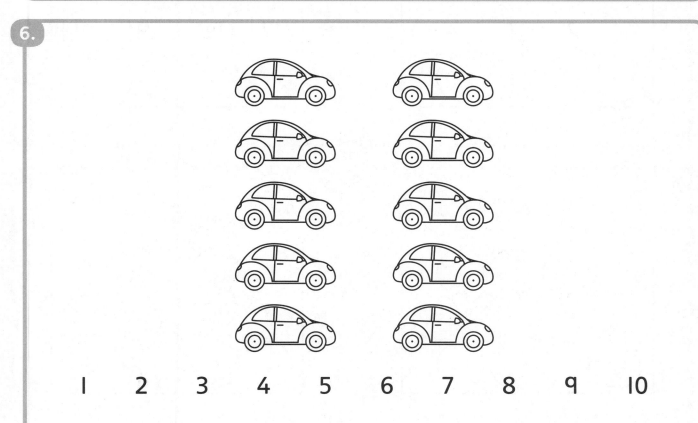

1   2   3   4   5   6   7   8   9   10

☐ Show counting out.

7.

5

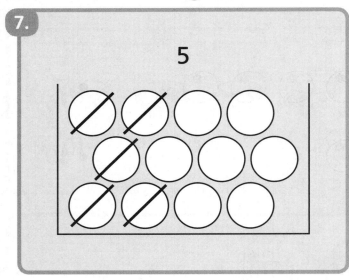

8.

8

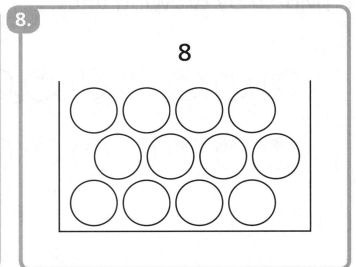

9.

7

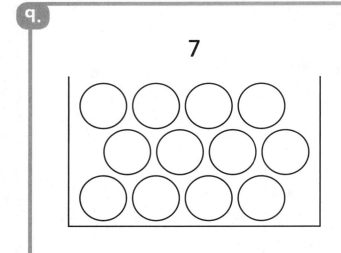

10.

q

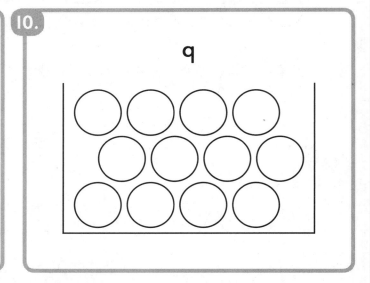

11.

10

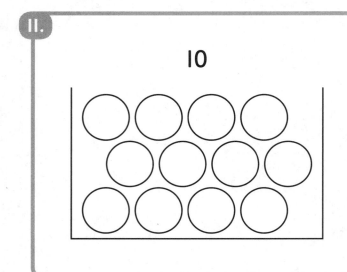

12.

6

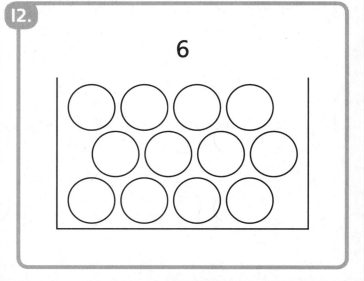

NSK-33 **The Number 10**

 Match by drawing lines.

1.
 • 7

• 10

2.
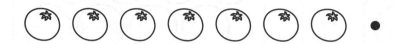 • 8

• q

3.
 • 10

• 8

4.
 • q

• 7

☐ Match by drawing lines.

5.

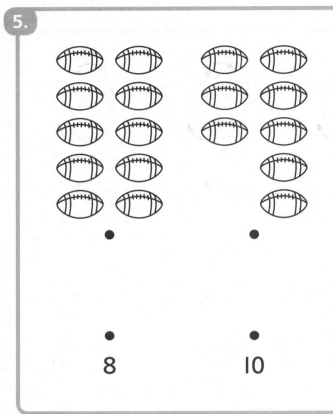

8   10

6.

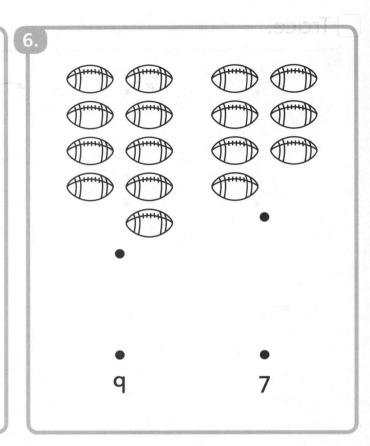

q   7

7.

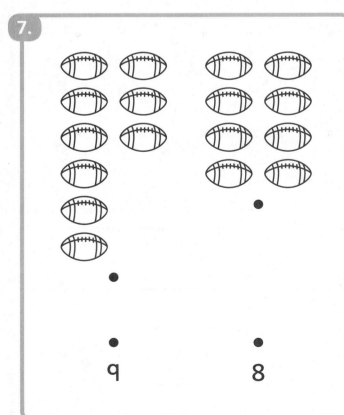

q   8

8.

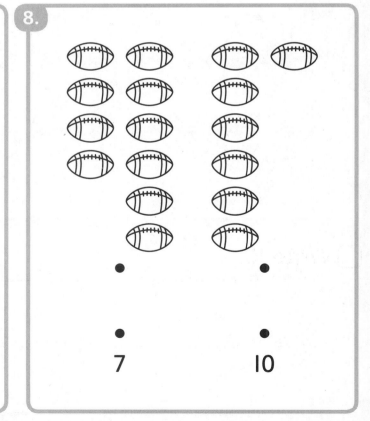

7   10

NSK-34 Writing 10

☐ Trace.

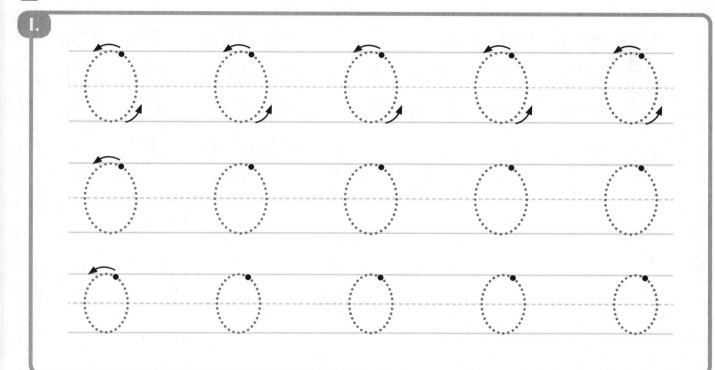

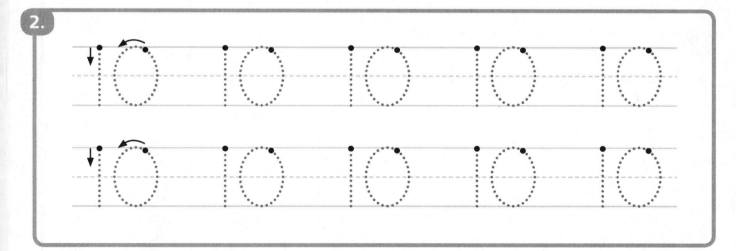

☐ Write 10.

3.

_____

- -

_____

☐ Trace.

4.

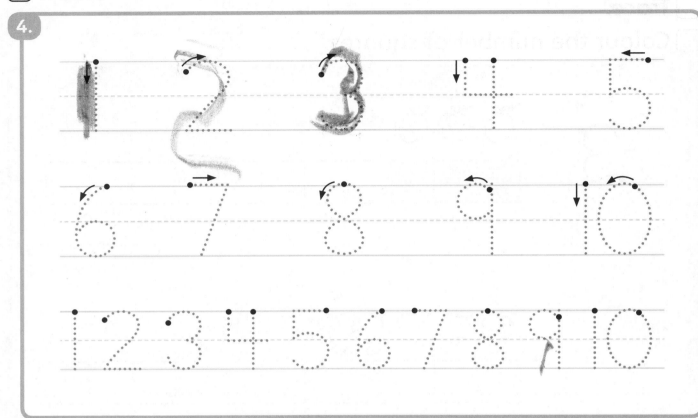

5.

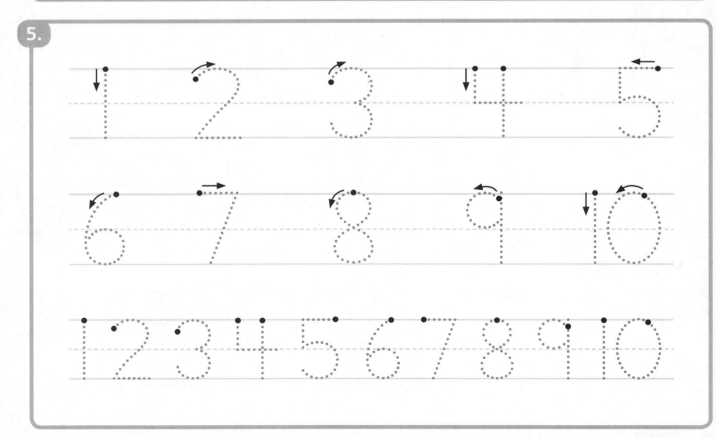

NSK-35 Review of 0 to 10

☐ Trace.
☐ Colour the number of squares.

1.
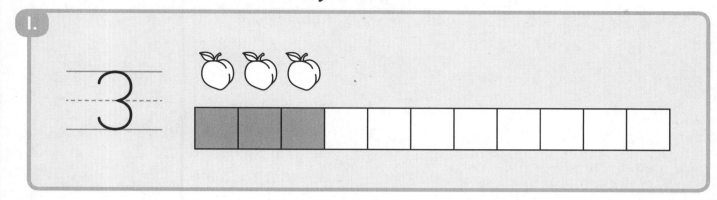

2.

3.
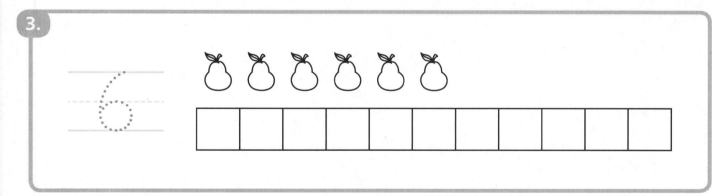

4.
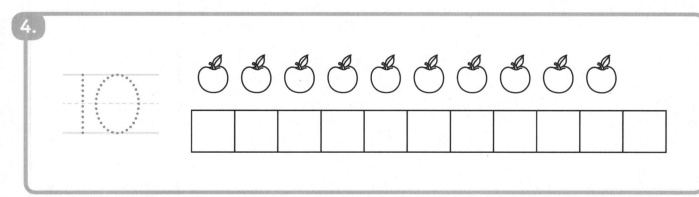

NSK-36 Counting to 60

☐ Trace.

1.

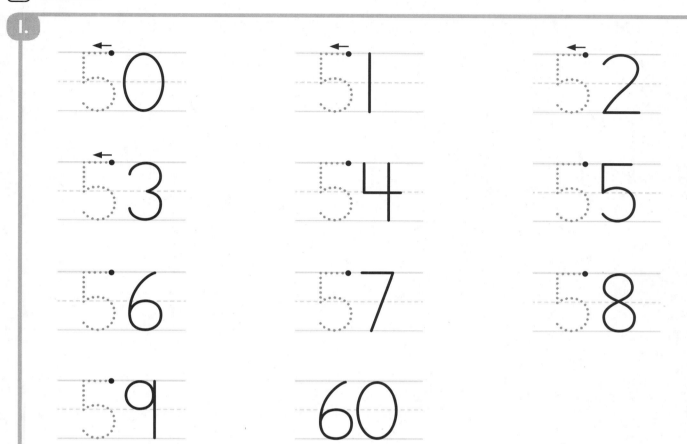

50 51 52
53 54 55
56 57 58
59 60

2.

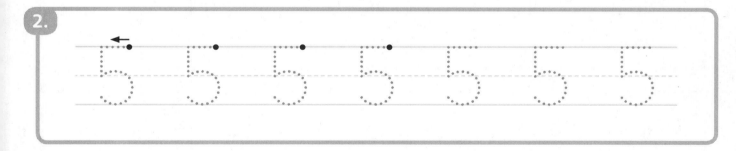

5 5 5 5 5 5 5

☐ Write 5.

3.

NSK-37 The Same Number (Equal)

☐ Match by drawing lines.
☐ Colour 😊 for the same. Colour ☹ for not the same.

1.

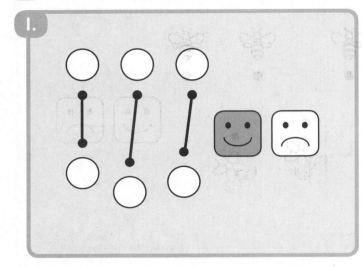

2.

3.

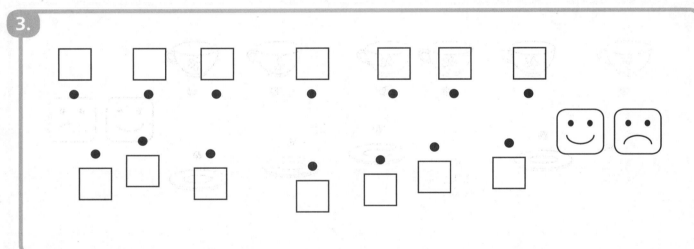

4.

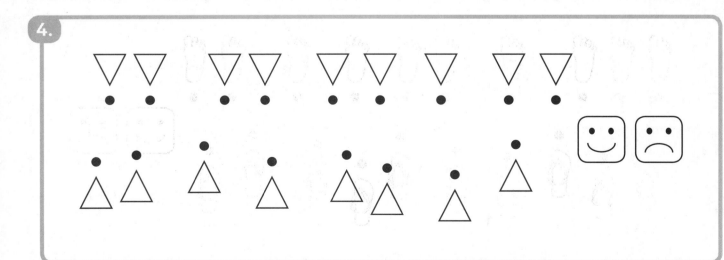

☐ Match by drawing lines.
☐ Colour 🙂 for the same. Colour 🙁 for not the same.

5.

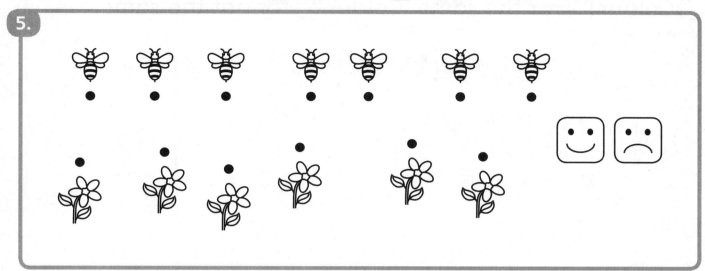

6.

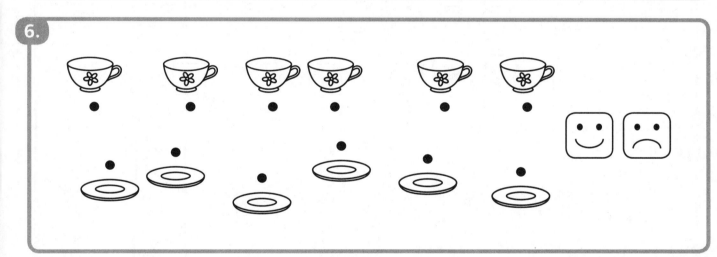

7.

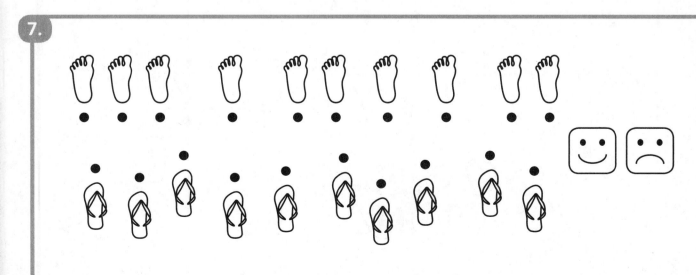

Count. Circle the number.
Colour  for the same. Colour for not the same.

8.

1   2   3   4   5   6   7   8   9   10

1   2   3   4   5   6   7   8   9   10

9.

1   2   3   4   5   6   7   8   9   10

1   2   3   4   5   6   7   8   9   10

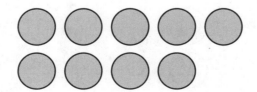

☐ Count. Circle the number.
☐ Colour 😊 for the same. Colour ☹ for not the same.

10.

1   2   3   4   5   6   7   8   9   10

1   2   3   4   5   6   7   8   9   10

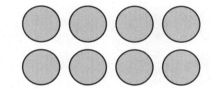

11.

1   2   3   4   5   6   7   8   9   10

1   2   3   4   5   6   7   8   9   10

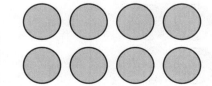

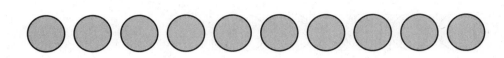
Count. Circle the number.
Colour ☺ for the same. Colour ☹ for not the same.

12.

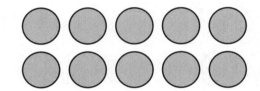

1   2   3   4   5   6   7   8   9   10

1   2   3   4   5   6   7   8   9   10

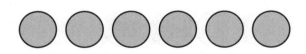

13.

1   2   3   4   5   6   7   8   9   10

1   2   3   4   5   6   7   8   9   10

Number Sense K-37

Count. Circle the number.
 Colour 🙂 for the same. Colour 🙁 for not the same.

14.

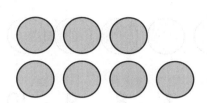

1   2   3   4   5   6   7   8   9   10

1   2   3   4   5   6   7   8   9   10

15. BONUS

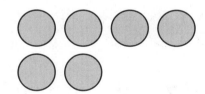

1   2   3   4   5   6   7   8   9   10

1   2   3   4   5   6   7   8   9   10

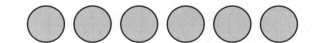

☐ Match by drawing lines.
☐ Colour the ☼ for the group that has more.

1.

2.

3.

☐ Match by drawing lines.
☐ Colour the ☼ for the group that has more.

4.

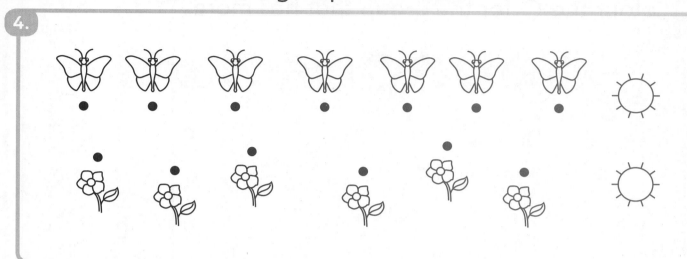

5.

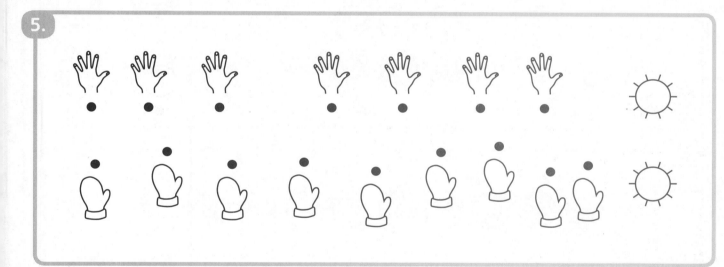

6.

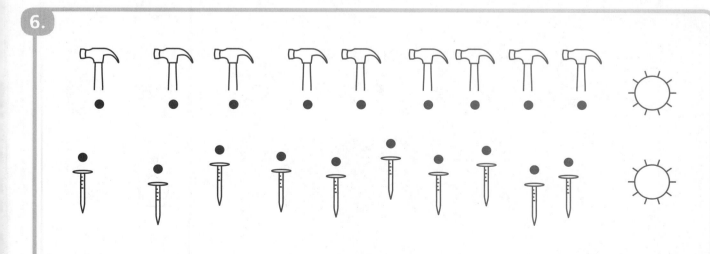

☐ Count. Circle the number.
☐ Colour the ☼ for the greater number.

7.

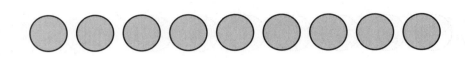

1   2   3   4   5   6   7   8   9   10

1   2   3   4   5   6   7   8   9   10

8.

1   2   3   4   5   6   7   8   9   10

1   2   3   4   5   6   7   8   9   10

Number Sense K-38

☐ Count. Circle the number.
☐ Colour the ☼ for the greater number.

9.

1   2   3   4   5   6   7   8   9   10

1   2   3   4   5   6   7   8   9   10

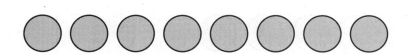

10.

1   2   3   4   5   6   7   8   9   10

1   2   3   4   5   6   7   8   9   10

□ Count. Circle the number.
□ Colour the ☼ for the greater number.

11.

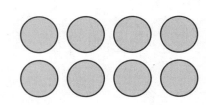

1   2   3   4   5   6   7   8   9   10

1   2   3   4   5   6   7   8   9   10   ☼

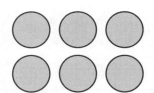

12.

1   2   3   4   5   6   7   8   9   10   ☼

1   2   3   4   5   6   7   8   9   10

☐ Count. Circle the number.
☐ Colour the ☼ for the greater number.

13. BONUS

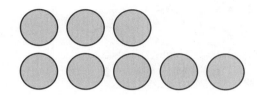

| 1 | 2 | 3 | 4 | 5 | 6 | 7 | 8 | 9 | 10 | ☼ |

| 1 | 2 | 3 | 4 | 5 | 6 | 7 | 8 | 9 | 10 | ☼ |

14. BONUS

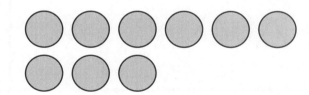

| 1 | 2 | 3 | 4 | 5 | 6 | 7 | 8 | 9 | 10 | ☼ |

| 1 | 2 | 3 | 4 | 5 | 6 | 7 | 8 | 9 | 10 | ☼ |

NSK-39 Less Than

☐ Match by drawing lines.
☐ Colour the ☼ for the group that has fewer.

1.

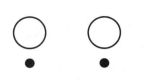  

2.

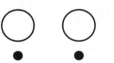

3.

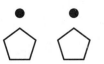   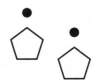

Match by drawing lines.
Colour the ☼ for the group that has fewer.

4.

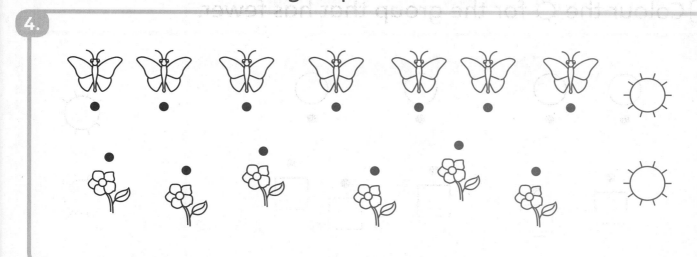

5.

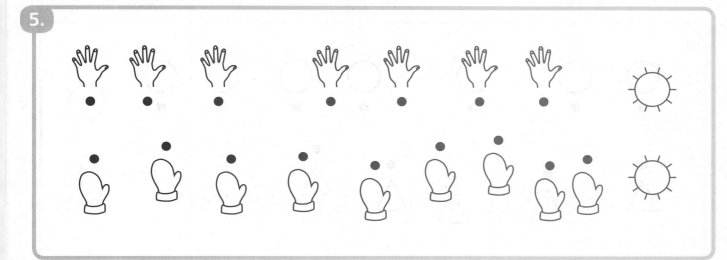

6.

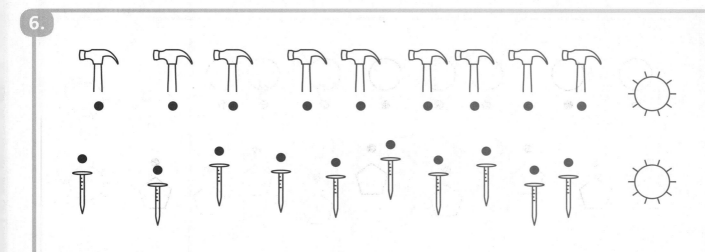

☐ Count. Circle the number.
☐ Colour the ☼ for the number that is less.

7.

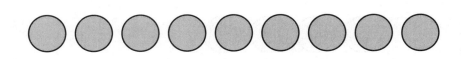

1   2   3   4   5   6   7   8   9   10

1   2   3   4   5   6   7   8   9   10

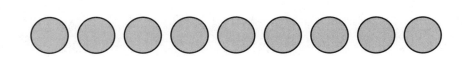

8.

1   2   3   4   5   6   7   8   9   10   ☼

1   2   3   4   5   6   7   8   9   10

☐ Count. Circle the number.
☐ Colour the ☀ for the number that is less.

9.

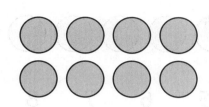

1   2   3   4   5   6   7   8   9   10   ☀

1   2   3   4   5   6   7   8   9   10   ☀

10.

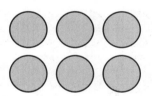

1   2   3   4   5   6   7   8   9   10   ☀

1   2   3   4   5   6   7   8   9   10   ☀

☐ Count. Circle the number.
☐ Colour the ☼ for the number that is less.

11.

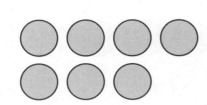

1   2   3   4   5   6   7   8   9   10

1   2   3   4   5   6   7   8   9   10

12.

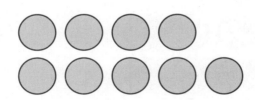

1   2   3   4   5   6   7   8   9   10

1   2   3   4   5   6   7   8   9   10

☐ Count. Circle the number.
☐ Colour the ☼ for the number that is less.

13. BONUS

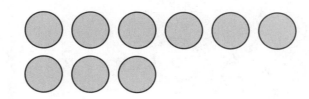

1   2   3   4   5   6   7   8   9   10   ☼

1   2   3   4   5   6   7   8   9   10   ☼

14. BONUS

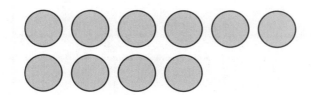

1   2   3   4   5   6   7   8   9   10   ☼

1   2   3   4   5   6   7   8   9   10   ☼

NSK-40 One More Than

☐ Draw a line below the number.
☐ Circle the next number.

1.

| 4 | 1 2 3 <u>4</u> ⑤ 6 7 8 9 10 |

2.

| 9 | 1 2 3 4 5 6 7 8 9 10 |

3.

| 5 | 1 2 3 4 5 6 7 8 9 10 |

4.

| 2 | 1 2 3 4 5 6 7 8 9 10 |

5.

| 8 | 1 2 3 4 5 6 7 8 9 10 |

☐ Match by drawing lines.
☐ Circle the extra ◯.
☐ Write how many extra.

6.

6   7

_____
- - - - - - - - -
_____

7.

4   5

_____
- - - - - - - - -
_____

8.

7   8

_____
- - - - - - - - -
_____

☐ Write the next number.
☐ Colour to show the next number.

9.

4   ⎯⎯⎯

10.

5   ⎯⎯⎯

11.

9   ⎯⎯⎯

☐ Write the next number.
☐ Colour to show the next number.

12.

8   --------

13.

6   --------

14.

7   --------

NSK-41 Comparing Numbers

☐ Circle the numbers.
☐ Colour the ☼ for the greater number.

1.

7 ☼

2 ☼

1   2   3   4   5   6   7   8   9   10

2.

3 ☼

9 ☼

1   2   3   4   5   6   7   8   9   10

3.

10 ☼

1 ☼

1   2   3   4   5   6   7   8   9   10

4.

4 ☼

6 ☼

1   2   3   4   5   6   7   8   9   10

☐ Colour to show the numbers. Match.
☐ Circle the number that is less.

5.
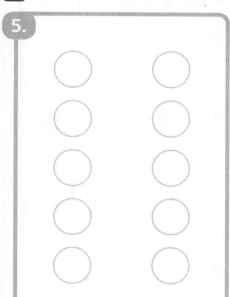

1   4

6.

4   2

7.
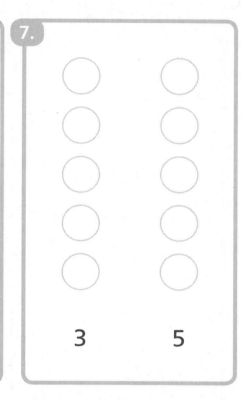

3   5

8.
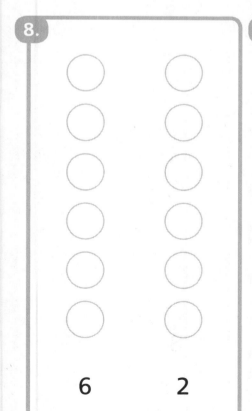

6   2

9.

3   6

10.

1   5

☐ Colour to show the numbers. Match.
☐ Circle the greater number.

11.	12.	13.

11.

9   5

12.

8   3

13.

6   10